CD-ROM

Also from
Blueprint Publishing

The Print and Production Manual
The Print and Production Manual Practical Kit
Magazine and Journal Production
The Web Offset Directory
Screen Process Printing: a practical guide

The Publisher's Guide Series
- **Desktop Publishing**
- **Litho Printing**
- **Typesetting and Composition**
- **Copy Prep**
- **Interfacing Word Processors and Phototypesetters**

Publisher's Guide Series

CD-ROM

Tony Feldman

BLUEPRINT

First published in the United Kingdom 1987 by
Blueprint Publishing Ltd
40 Bowling Green Lane
London EC1R 0NE
Tel. 01 278 0333

British Library Cataloguing in Publication Data
Feldman, Tony
CD-ROM.——(Publisher's guide series).
1. Publishers and publishing——Data processing 2. Compact discs. 3. Read-only storage
I. Title II. Series
004.5′6 QA76

ISBN 0 948905 10 7

Keyed by the author on an Amstrad PCW 8256
Formatted, paginated and output by Text Generation Ltd, London WC2B
Printed by Antony Rowe Ltd, Chippenham, Wiltshire

Contents

Introduction

Today new technologies suffer from their own cleverness. When Neil Armstrong stepped onto the surface of the moon, a TV audience of millions on Earth held their breath. The romance of the moment, its drama and sense of history, was a mixture of many things. For most, the miracle of seeing a man standing on the surface of another world, almost a quarter of a million miles away, was compounded both of the heroism of the astronaut and the awesome technological ingenuity which carried him to the moon and enabled us to watch while he took those dramatic first steps. It was a time when technological achievement still caught the imagination and could be embraced equally with such human qualities as courage and endurance.

Since the flight of Apollo 11, the romance has faded. We have been so swamped by wave after wave of new technology that it sometimes feels as if we are all drowning in its cleverness. Computers do things so complex we can barely understand them. Devices store more information than we can comfortably comprehend. Telecommunication links network the world. A whole culture of smart acronyms and fancy terms has sprung up to baffle and amaze. And, naturally, everything happens at the speed of light. Who can fail to be overwhelmed by the cleverness of it all? But like a dog dancing on one leg, it is wonderful, even awe-inspiring, but utterly meaningless if we cannot see some practical purpose for it.

So new technologies have to do more than just clever tricks. In particular, if we are generic publishers — that is to say we publish for broadly based markets — the technologies have to do something with information that enables us to make products we can sell —

and sell at a profit. Above all else, this guide addresses this single issue. It is not about using technology to help us produce books or to run our businesses more efficiently. It is about creating products in the medium of the technology itself; products that make some bottom-line sense.

Interpreting any technology as a publishing medium needs one very important thing. It needs demystification. Like a modern day Cabbala, it is cloaked in arcane terms and allusions. It also embodies some genuinely difficult scientific and engineering concepts. But like most things, there is a huge difference between what there is to know about technology and what you need to know.

The key to demystification is simple. Do not try to understand everything. Acquire enough of a grasp of how a technology works to be able to concentrate on what it can do. Once you can see its real-life applications, the spell is broken. Technology is just another tool and like any tool, its importance is in its use. The process of demystification is complete. You are in control and can take decisions using the same principles of commonsense which have always applied in good publishing.

This is a book specifically about optical discs and, more specifically still, it is about the so-called 'compact disc read only memory', (CD-ROM). If new technology suffers from its cleverness, CD-ROM suffers from its name. It hardly has the panache of some of the more glamorous jargon terms. So why CD-ROM? The answer is simple. Optical disc technology used under computer control seems to offer most of the features of a book together with real benefits a book cannot offer. So the interactive, randomly accessed optical disc looks like a high-tech but superior analogue of a book. For this reason it attracts publishers. After all, over the centuries, the book has been the most profitable information product of all time. The possibility of coming up with something similar but better just has to be taken seriously.

Words like 'interactive' and 'randomly accessed', used casually in the last paragraph, need considerable attention. They are two of the keys to the power of optical disc technology as a publishing medium. We cannot take them lightly and later chapters will discuss them in some detail.

As far as this book is concerned, CD-ROM and associated media are publishing, not technological, issues. This is not therefore a work of great technical insight. I am a non-technically minded generic publisher writing for other non-technically minded generic publishers. The experts can have some fun finding rough edges in what follows if they like but they will be missing the point. My subject is publishing and the strategy of publishing. Nothing else.

If we have to take in some technical know-how along the way, we will try to do it without the mystery. I cannot guarantee that the journey will be entirely painless but I hope it will be worth making. Whether we are fearful that these new methods of delivering information may undermine our more traditional publishing markets or whether we see them offering new avenues for profitable investment, we must be in a position to evaluate the possibilities. Is CD-ROM a threat, an opportunity or an irrelevance? Whatever decision a publisher takes about getting involved or staying out, it must be taken from a position of knowledge not ignorance. This book sets out to offer publishers the high ground from which they can work out their CD-ROM strategy and ultimately succeed in whatever battle they choose to fight.

For my mother and for Deborah, two ladies
who (thankfully) care nothing for CD-ROM

1

New Media Publishing

In this first chapter we will touch upon some important underlying ideas in any publishing appraisal of the new media. To start with, a warning, followed by a plea for healthy scepticism. Then an application of the publisher's most reliable friend: the 'so what?' test. Finally, an examination of our options in assessing markets that are so young, their patterns and characteristics are as yet unformed.

First, however, we need to be clear about some terms. 'New technology' and 'new media' are today widely and carelessly used phrases. They often mean slightly different things in different contexts. In all that follows here, 'new technology' is the hardware and software tools that embody the 'new media' and enable us to use it. The term 'new media' itself means computer-accessed information. In particular, this guide is focused on the medium created by connecting the control facilities of a computer to the storage and access facilities of a CD-ROM. Much of what will be said is more general than this and has wider significance but our principal focus, whatever the generalities, is the implications for publishers of plugging a computer into an optical disc drive. If you are particularly rigorous you may notice 'new technology' and 'new media' being used interchangeably but hopefully this will not stand in the way of the meaning of the text.

What can be, will be

Physics does not like dealing with philosophy. It has a touch of disdain for all things metaphysical. If a phenomenon cannot be measured we cannot know anything meaningful about it, so why bother with it in the first place? But whether physics likes it or not, it does contain some deeply philosophical ideas. One of the few I still remember is more or less expressed by that classic old song 'Que Sera, Sera'. Except physics changes one word in the lyrics. Instead of saying 'what will be, will be', physics says 'what can be, will be'.

For example, physics teaches us that a gas like the air is composed of millions of tiny particles called molecules, hurtling about in a violent random movement. They constantly collide with one another and other objects. This is called the kinetic theory of gases. The only way we can get to grips with the mêlée of microscopic movement is by using mathematical techniques called 'statistical analysis'. This means that while we cannot predict how an individual molecule will behave, we can say something statistically about the behaviour of the whole gas.

Statistics is about saying how probable it is that events will occur. The mathematical measure involved is called 'probability'. Probability comes in all sizes and some are very small indeed. So there is a small but finite chance that while you are reading these words, all the air molecules in your room will simultaneously rush into one corner. You will then die horribly of asphyxiation. But do not panic. The chance is so tiny that you are much more likely to be struck by a meteorite.

So physics embraces all events whose probability of occurring is greater than zero. But it goes further. Not only can the improbable happen, it will happen. If you wait long enough, sometime, somewhere the least likely things in the universe will take place. Those monkeys tapping away at their typewriters, will eventually write the entire works of Shakespeare. Unless an event is forbidden by a fundamental natural law, it will occur. In other words: 'what can be, will be'.

The notion of things that are possible always happening in the end, plays a big role in the way people see the future. When H.G. Wells wrote *Things to Come*, he foresaw a future of remorseless technological advance, one in which ultimately, to escape the implications of that advance, men had to flee their own planet. The modern fantasy writer, Ray Bradbury, in an interlude in his epic, *Martian Chronicles*, pictured a future world of total automation. His haunting image was of an Earth deserted by its population. All that remained were empty homes that continued a kind of robot parody of life. Radios and televisions were still turned on and off, rooms were dusted, windows cleaned, lawns mowed and all by automated machines. The everyday activities of middle-class life went on without a single living person within a million miles.

This way of seeing the future is a conscious or unconscious statement of the principle 'what can be, will be'. As far as physics is concerned, the principle seems to work well. But it breaks down dramatically when we try to apply it to human beings and what they do with their society. Most important, as far as we are concerned in this book, it breaks down when used to predict technological change.

A commonplace reaction to emerging technologies is that they are inevitably the stuff of tomorrow. If you are directly involved in publishing and using new technology, you may find yourself described as being on the 'leading edge' of the business. You will be told you are the future of the industry or that you are 'pushing the envelope' and moving into exciting and fruitful new fields. The basic feeling behind all this is that the old established media of communication must sooner or later be displaced by the dazzling newcomers. Specifically and most wildly of all, you will be told that the time of the book is almost over. People will read things only from screens, head-up displays built into their spectacles or even via microchips plugged directly into their heads! Paper is an outmoded medium for communication, crude and inefficient, jamming up filing cabinets and desks. (Most of this helpful information will of course reach you on the outmoded medium itself!)

Whether the people saying these things know it or not, they are falling into the 'what can be, will be' trap. A few years ago similar sentiments might have been expressed to the designers and builders of the first supersonic passenger aircraft. Today Concorde languishes on the pages of luxury holiday brochures and while a modest number of toppish people zoom back and forth at 1400 miles an hour, the majority go for solid, sensible 'old technology', like the familiar Jumbo Jet. Some years earlier, the US Apollo project, according to its publicity handouts, was set to take mankind on a new era of interplanetary travel. The frightening thing about this was that the NASA organisation actually believed its own publicity. Now we see manned space flight in a more modest and much truer perspective, an element in the overall scheme of space exploration.

It seems there is a single acid test for these and many other technological developments: can the technology be sold?

This is perhaps an over-simplification, but it sets up a guide for publishers considering the future of information products. The ultimate arbiter of technological change is economic. At some level, the numbers have to work. Whatever else we think of the US 'Star Wars' initiative, for example, it is based on economics as much as politics. The billions of dollars spent will revitalise industry and encourage research and development leading to yet more commercially viable technology.

The world of the science fiction writer or the starry-eyed futurologist who think it is only a matter of time before this or that is invented and a part of everyday life, is not and never will be the real world. And above all else, publishers have to live in the real world, seeing things as they are and not as publishers would want them to be. So the first key lesson in publishing in the media of the new technologies is that their cleverness is not enough. They have to do something with information that is both different from traditional media and relevant to the needs of information users. This must add up to something for which people are prepared to pay. And the price must be enough to give you your profit margin.

As we see, the lesson for new media publishing is basically the same as for any publishing. Understand the market and get your publishing economics right. But when you are dealing with new media such as computer software, video discs or CD-ROMs, there is a danger of believing the chorus of voices that say 'these are the books of tomorrow'. They may be and, if they are, you could get very rich by investing right away. However, test your strategy in the same stringent way as any publishing project. What is the market? What is your product? How will you distribute it? How many? How much? At all costs avoid technology intoxication. It dims the senses and ruins businesses. There are plenty of voices out there encouraging you to drink up the heady words about explosive market growths. Some come from people who make money simply if you invest; the parasitic new technology support industry. Listen more to the people who make money if you invest and make a profit. Above all, forget 'what can be, will be'.

This is a plea not to believe the supposed promise of new technology publishing just because it is exciting, different and clever. It may seem too obvious to put into words — except that there are a lot of normally very level-headed publishers at large saying very unlevel-headed things. There is also a pseudo-momentum built up by the support industries that live off both the possibility and the actuality of publishing investment in these fields. Every potential new media spawns journals, newsletters and books (like this one!). Alongside these are the facilities companies. If you want to make a video disc, CD-ROM or even a CD-I disc, there are plenty of companies ready to do it all for you as a package deal. However, they will, on the whole, be happier with a contract fee rather than royalties on your sales! If these are the sources of information for evaluating the potential new markets, you must be alert to the fact that a very large axe is being ground. A good dose of healthy scepticism is essential to distinguish the subjective from the objective in what is written and said.

So how can a publisher hope to assess new media markets? Certainly there are very real problems both because the voices of unreason are so loud and because the markets are, by definition, embryonic. But perhaps before addressing this issue, the publisher should answer an even more basic question: why bother in the first place? What is really so special about new technology? Does it pass the 'so what?' test?

What's new about new technology?

For centuries, the term 'publisher' has referred to people who made and distributed books, journals, magazines, newspapers. Basically the same meaning is being placed on the word throughout this book. Such an activity is a generic one with products which are being designed for a broad type of audience rather than individuals.

This has always been a straightforward and workable way of seeing publishing. So why do computers and optical discs change anything? The answer is that they may not. Perhaps publishers can resolutely ignore the whole field of computer-accessed information and carry on just producing good books. However, we need to recognise that technology now offers powerful new ways of handling a range of different kinds of information. In itself, this is not enough to explain why publishers should bother with them. After all, there have been other big developments in the information business before now. The movie industry, radio and television: none were signals for publishers to diversify their business and convey information using these new media. What then is different now? We could spend a lot of time over the analysis but the most important answer is 'information access'.

Television is a wonderful medium but it is better at entertaining people than informing them. In terms of information technology, television has two major constraints. First, its transmissions start at the beginning and go on to the end. In other words, they are linear. Second, there is nothing the viewer can do to change the transmission. It is essentially a passive process of communication. The same applies to radio and to movies.

The difference between these old media and the new, is that the new ones are neither linear nor passive. If we concentrate just on computers and optical discs, we can see immediately that the key to their power as information tools is the way the information product which they embody can be accessed. As we will see when we examine how these systems work, it is possible to pull out data from the information base in any sequence or, indeed, in no sequence whatsoever. Because of this, it is possible for the user to interrogate the information in many different ways and so discover a range of different paths through the material. This returns us to those two key concepts mentioned in the opening paragraphs of this book: random access and interactivity. They are the opposites of the linear, passive access which characterises so many established media.

It is hard to overestimate the importance of these two features in the potential new generation of information products and it is vital to recognise that together they represent a new kind of communication vehicle, perhaps of unprecedented power. After all, in every field of experience, the way we access and interact with available information fundamentally affects the outcome. This is as true of the school classroom as it is of the office of a multi-national company. It is as true for the champion chess player as it is for the fighter pilot locked in a high-speed dogfight. Whatever we do we are constantly interpreting data and that means issues of access and interaction.

What of the book? Why should publishers look further than the information product that has best stood the test of time in every imaginable information field? Indeed, the book is a powerful medium in its own right. It may not have the glamour of the new technologies but it does a remarkable job cheaply and well and it is portable. It also has the benefit of a kind of cultural acceptability. This means more than saying we are comfortable with books. They are a part of our social fabric. The process of using books and documents has been so well learned by most of humankind, we have forgotten that any particular skills are involved. Yet the scanning of pages, the flicking between pages, the use of indexes and systems of headings involve very sophisticated skills. We just know them so well, we have forgotten they exist. The 'technology' of the book is transparent to the reader. The reader does not notice any technique in getting in touch with the information the book contains. The reader just reads.

In this sense the book is light years ahead of computer-accessed information. Faced with keyboards, keypads, screens and the paraphernalia of hardware that computer-based information technology needs, most of the uninitiated understandably feel insecure. Even the more experienced users generally have to employ skills consciously to 'read' their technological book. There is no transparency about this technology. So the medium can get in the way of the message.

However, if we consider the potential nature of that message, the traditional book is decidedly on less sure ground. First, the message can be huge. As we will see, a CD-ROM or similar medium can contain about six hundred million printed characters. This means, for example, that all of the telephone directories in use in Europe could be stored on just two discs! Second, the access to this vast storehouse of information is fast and random. Typically, any of the information on a CD-ROM can be located and retrieved in less than a second.

So even if books are cheaper, more portable and culturally acceptable, faced with the dramatic potential of computer-accessed information, publishers must look carefully at the market opportunities. It has to be taken seriously. Publishers need to bother.

Evaluating the markets

How do you evaluate something that may not yet exist? In the world of print-based publishing, there exist established markets. We know more or less how many copies different types of book or journal will sell. In educational publishing, for example, list-building can become almost mechanical. Examine syllabuses, examination candidate numbers, check competing publications and find the right people to write for you. It is easy. There are rules. In trade publishing, the rules are fewer and the game is more exciting. But there are still fixed points. Books on cats and dinosaurs are likely to be steady sellers. Books written by the kings and queens of mass-market fiction will be big sellers if you get your publicity right, have the channels of distribution and a big enough cheque book to buy the properties in the first place.

This simplified portrait of a complex and challenging industry highlights the intrinsic problem of totally new kinds of information products. In the new media, the rules have still to be written. The customers, the end-users of the new types of product, are not clearly defined. All aspects of the familiar publishing processes have to be re-assessed. What should the subject be? How do we author the product? How is it manufactured, priced, marketed, distributed?

There are two approaches to this problem: you either lead or you follow. Leading is, of course, the boldest option and means you set out to establish the market by direct experience. You gather together all the data you can, draw up all the publishing know-how and intuition you can muster, and leap in. Following is a more cautious approach and only gives you market knowledge based on other people's experience. Moreover, if the market is a fast-mover, the choicest fruits may have already been plucked by the leaders.

In reality, of course, there are middle grounds to be found. You can be a following leader or a leading follower and find a balance that suits the degree of risk you find acceptable. Indeed, risk strategy is a key issue here. Any publisher approaching new media investment must budget that operation in a special way. Realism is essential. There is little point in letting your new media operation sit on the corporate budget in the same way as your school or college publishing lists. There must be a corporate admission that massively more risk is inherent in examining and developing these embryonic markets. Cost and revenue forecasts are bound to be less reliable than in any established area of the business. Big allowances need to be built into the figures to reflect an uncertainty that is inherent in this kind of publishing. The word 'inherent' needs real emphasis. The degree of risk in this kind of investment is not fundamentally a question of the publisher's skill as a publisher. This obviously matters and a good publisher always stands a better chance of success than a bad one. But in approaching new media investment there is a vagueness about market characteristics that no amount of research and analysis can remove.

If we can swallow this bitter pill and still get a budget for new media publishing, there remains the problem of some kind of useful market evaluation. At the time of writing, there are already some 'leaders' in the field whose publishing approach and experience can be examined. Commercial generic CD-ROM products, for example, are already in three figures worldwide so there are a good number of CD-ROM publishers already actively swopping punches with the problems and uncertainties of the market. There are some basic raw data available on such issues as hardware bases by application area. In other words, some of the normal evaluation procedures familiar to good publishing practice can be applied even to such an embryonic market place. Statistics can be uncovered, costs can be obtained, marketing and distribution models exist. What has to be recognised is the uncertainty in them all. These statistics are more unreliable than most. Costings can easily be misunderstood and vital but expensive steps in production or pre-production overlooked. Finally, the benefits, pitfalls and overall effectiveness of the publishing models are still largely untested.

Where does this leave us? You can know something about the market but you cannot rely on the information. It is all very risky but it helps to be a good publisher. What kind of practical guideline is this?

Perhaps the most fundamental guideline is to decide to start where all good publishing starts: with the customers, the people who will actually exchange their money for your product hoping to get some worthwhile benefit from it. Sometimes these people know what they want and we only need to find out what it is. Sometimes they do not know what they want but recognise a good thing when they see it. We only need to anticipate what they would recognise as a good thing. These are publishing commonplaces, familiar and tested. So why not use the same approach in new media publishing? Clearly some preparatory analysis is needed. We need to understand the capabilities of the medium in which we want to publish. We need to decide broadly on the market sectors in which we think we may find potential: business, education, training or even the home. But, most crucially of all, we need to know our customers.

If we already publish successfully in traditional media for the chosen market sectors, we should know a good deal about our customers. Editors, after all, should not merely be responsive to markets. If they are good at their jobs, they are actively engaged with them, understanding clearly how customers use the information or entertainment products that have already been successfully published. For example, if editors are in touch with the market for scientific reference material, they should have a good grasp of how the information products are used, their value to customers in different modes of use and the likely future trends in the way such customers may want information presented. With this basis of knowledge, we have the most important market evaluation of all. Developing the new media product for the market is then a creative issue and is a challenge to the creative skills of publishers. It cannot of course be an editorial process alone. Major issues of cost, marketing and distribution have to be addressed. But the primary issue is the target customers' needs and the value they place on an information product that answers those needs.

2

What is an Optical Disc?

To understand a new media product we have to steel ourselves for some coverage of the technology. While publishers have no need to become experts on the underlying technicalities, they do need to know what an optical disc is and what it is capable of doing. This chapter aims to keep things simple and concentrate on optical disc basics.

Origins and development

Sometimes evolution and revolution look the same. It is just a question of pace. When evolution takes place very swiftly, it looks much the same as a sudden, spontaneous explosion of change. The word 'revolution' is certainly worked hard in the field of computers and optical discs. This is only because so much has happened so fast, but, in fact, no matter how radical they are, all developments have their antecedents.

Not surprisingly then, the optical disc was invented long before Neil Armstrong stepped onto the moon. It even pre-dates the first digital computers. In fact a patent for a video disc was filed in 1927, almost ten years before the first commercial television broadcast. The video disc pioneer was the Scottish inventor, John Logie Baird, better known for developing a prototype television system.

Baird called the disc technology 'Phonovision' and, as the name suggests, it owed a lot to contemporary gramophones. The video disc itself was made of the brittle plastic of ordinary audio records and was played on a modified gramophone linked to one of Baird's Televisor receivers. The result on the Televisor's screen, was up to a dozen, low quality still images. Baird actually went on to sell pre-recorded video discs under a label he called 'Radiovision'. However, the technology was a commercial failure and was forgotten as soon as modern electronic television systems were introduced.

The real breakthrough in video disc technology happened in the United States in 1960. Theodore Maiman applied the research and design suggestions of fellow scientist, Charles Townes, and built the first laser.

While we do not need to know much about laser physics, it is helpful to keep in mind what a laser can do. Basically it is a kind of light 'gun'. It is loaded by being pumped up with electrical and magnetic energy. When the trigger is pulled, the laser fires a pencil-thin beam of very pure light. The light emitted is extraordinary for three reasons. First, instead of containing many different frequencies like light from conventional sources, laser light contains just a single frequency. Rather like a great singer, the laser has perfect pitch and consistently sings a single note of total purity. Second, the light beam can be focused with pinpoint accuracy onto microscopically small targets. Third, laser light is extremely intense and while its power to damage can be readily controlled, it can, if necessary, punch a hole in a steel plate.

Amongst its many applications, the laser was destined to become the stylus with which most future optical discs would be played. Indeed, Philips paid the most eloquent tribute to laser technology by naming their first commercial video disc system 'LaserVision'. The laser now lies at the heart of optical disc technology and many of the discs' most important features depend on the laser's remarkable characteristics as well as on the ability (even more remarkable) of today's producers to make lasers small, cheap, reliable and in mass market volumes.

The laser video disc is the forerunner of CD-ROM and, through understanding how video discs work, we can get to grips with some important features of compact discs. They have many generic similarities and one fundamental difference.

How a video disc works

The audio gramophone record is a useful analogue of the video disc. We are all familiar with the plastic recordings of music that remain today a huge worldwide leisure industry. The single long spiral groove on a record carries in it mechanical wiggles that create vibrations in a stylus that tracks swiftly through it. Gramophones work by spinning the disc at a constant number of revolutions per minute while the stylus passes along the groove. The vibrations set up in the stylus are converted into an electrical signal which changes in its intensity with the changes in the vibrations. This rapidly varying signal is cleaned up, amplified and converted into audible sound through a speaker. In this way the mechanical variations in the surface of the disc are preserved through a number of key stages. First they are detected and converted into a varying electrical current. Then the variations are amplified. Finally, they are re-converted into a mechanically varying signal in the form of sound. Throughout, the information, whether the music of Dire Straits or J.S. Bach, is being conveyed by something that is constantly varying. Information conveyed in this way is said to be analogue information (*see* page 17).

In the laser video disc, the information needed to make a video picture is coded in a similar way. A stylus runs through a spiral track and detects mechanical variations in it. However much more information is needed to form video images than sound. To get even a single video frame, the spiral would have to be both extremely long and densely packed with mechanical variations. In order to play a video sequence, involving a large number of individual frames viewed sequentially, there has to be one long spiral track for each frame. So the problems of packing all this information on a disc are formidable. The solution is twofold. First change the plane of the spiral tracks from the horizontal to the vertical. Second, use a tiny laser as the stylus.

If you look at a video disc you will first be struck by its beautiful silvered appearance. Its surface is covered by a highly reflective aluminium layer that allows a beam of laser light to bounce off its surface with practically no loss of intensity. What you cannot easily see with the naked eye is the tightly packed spiral tracks covering the brilliant surface. Typically there can be as many as 54,000 of them. If you examined any of the tracks through a powerful microscope you would see how the information is carried. Unlike an audio disc which has wiggles in the sides of the tracks, here you would see variations in the floor. A series of minute pits of varying sizes are etched into it. So if we imagine the track on an audio disc as a meandering river whose banks constantly wander from side to side, the video disc track is more like a steep and smooth-sided canyon with a bumpy floor along which the laser stylus hurtles.

A major advantage of a stylus made of light is that there is no mechanical contact with the surface of the disc. For this reason, neither the stylus nor the disc can ever wear out. Also, because a laser can be focused with pinpoint accuracy, it is possible to coat the disc surface with a clear plastic. This protects the disc from dust and scratches while the laser light penetrates it with ease, being brought to sharp focus on the very 'floor' of the information-carrying tracks. As the beam sweeps along that floor it identifies the pitted areas and the unpitted ones by the changes in how reflective the surface is. Practically all of the light is reflected from the highly reflective, unpitted sections. There is no loss of intensity in the light. But the pits are not so reflective and when the light strikes them, not all of it bounces back. So there is a drop in the intensity of the light for as long as it is moving over an area of pitted surface.

In this way, the fluctuating intensity of the laser beam measured at the 'head' of the stylus, records the lengths of the pits etched into the surface of the disc. The variation in the intensity contains the basic analogue information from which a video picture can be built. What happens next is simple. The variation in light intensity collected from the length of one of the thousands of tracks on the disc, is converted into an electrical signal which itself varies in intensity in the same way. This is then amplified and eventually decoded by some ingenious electronic circuitry and reconstructed on a television or monitor screen as a single video image.

We can make all this more concrete by examining a real video disc. The Philips LaserVision disc has a diameter of 12 inches. Together, its 54,000 spiral tracks contain enough information for a colour video programme with accompanying twin-track sound and control data to facilitate playback operations. Because Europe has a slightly different television system from the United States, European discs are spun at 1500 revolutions per minute compared with 1800 for their American counterparts. With one video frame per track, playing time is about thirty minutes on each side of the disc.

There are two types of playback available from most disc players. One is called 'Constant Angular Velocity' (CAV). The other is called 'Constant Linear Velocity' (CLV). Each has distinct features of enormous importance to the way in which information can be accessed from the disc.

CAV is sometimes called 'Active Play' because it enables users to take information from the disc in different ways. The name is a useful reminder that CLV is, by contrast, a largely 'passive' means of playback. In Active Play the disc spins at a constant rate and as the stylus is moved from the innermost to the outermost track, its speed of movement across the disc is increased. This is to enable the stylus to read a longer distance of track in the outer parts of the disc in the same time as it takes to read the shorter distance in the inner region.

Using this system of playback two crucial facilities are introduced. Since one track contains one video frame, we can freeze the image on a single frame by simply directing the stylus to scan one track continuously. Also, because we can control the speed and direction of the stylus, we can place an identifying 'number' in every video frame and then direct the stylus to locate and read any one of the 54,000 frames. With the right kind of control system attached to the stylus this kind of retrieval can be accomplished in a couple of seconds, sometimes substantially less.

The CLV or Long Play mode is offered to enable much more playing time to be drawn from a disc. While CAV with its random access facility looks exciting to people who need to use it, it is hardly an attractive feature for those who want to simply watch a linear video programme from beginning to end. In this case, the viewer is much more interested in the length of playback time he gets for his money. CAV with a single video frame per track is wasteful on space. The CLV approach is to pack each track with as many frames as it can take. On the outer part of the disc where the spiral is particularly long, for example, two or even three frames can be recorded. The frames are packed in as tightly as possible and the stylus tracking speed is kept constant. The speed of revolution of the disc is varied so that the stylus passes over each frame at the same speed. In this way the playing time of each side can be doubled to sixty minutes. The increase in playing time is traded off against the loss of freeze frame capabilities. It is also a much slower process to address a single frame of the video under CLV. Instead of locating a required frame by an electronically stored number, the frame is found by measuring the amount of time it takes in normal playback to reach the frame.

Active Play video discs have slowly found a range of applications where the random accessibility of video images is of real value. By placing the playback machine under computer control or even building a microprocessor into the machine itself, fully interactive video programming can be achieved. With the right hardware, information from the video disc can be combined and overlaid on a single screen with data generated by the computer. The potential for the areas of industrial, business, scientific and military simulations is huge. Add to this the opportunities for interactive programming for education, training, point of sale promotion and home entertainment and you might expect that the laser disc would be big business throughout the world. The market for interactive video products has certainly grown over the last few years but the scale of growth has been from tiny to very small. And the growth is exclusively in the bespoke market where individual information products have been created under contract for a client with particular needs. The generic market is effectively non-existent.

There are several reasons why this has happened. A major problem has been the persistent failure of interactive programme makers to deliver the goods. Too many video companies, more at home making boring corporate communications programmes, have tried to diversify into interactive video. Although many learned the jargon fluently, none could muster the creative power needed to make use of such a complex and demanding medium. It is a striking and depressing fact that if you visit the circus of seminars and so-called 'executive updates' about interactive video, you hear the same things being said today as were said five years ago. Interactive video programme makers have been going round in circles for years. They are getting fewer each year as more return to making the linear videos they understand best. Sadly they have already damaged the image of interactive video. Who can criticise companies, governments and education agencies who are writing off interactive video on the basis of the poor offerings they have so far seen?

A further reason for the slow growth of the market is cash. Interactive video is a costly medium so its benefits must be obvious in order to convince anyone to buy it. While there have been some big successes, many of those who have bought major interactive video systems are bitterly disappointed.

Most significantly for those of us looking anxiously at compact disc technology, interactive video has floundered because it uses a non-standard hardware configuration. The expensive disc players are often incompatible with one another and, ultimately, can do nothing else except play video discs. They represent a big commitment in financial terms, especially when not all the discs you can buy will fit your player! Compact disc technology has benefitted from a vital degree of standardisation from the outset. It has entered modern life through the music industry and in a matter of a few years, both discs and players are being manufactured in huge numbers all over the world. Although some players obviously have much more specialised applications than those which are vehicles for music recordings, the backdrop is of an essentially mass-market industry.

Analogue and digital information

Before we examine the main concern of this guide, the compact disc, it is important to emphasise a key division in the world of information.

Whether we know it or not, we are most familiar with a kind of information called analogue information. Most of this chapter has so far dealt with ways of detecting analogue information and converting it from one form to another. Throughout we characterised it by referring to constantly varying values: light intensities, the meanders in the audio record's groove, the variations in an electrical current, the mechanical fluctuations of air which we interpret as sound. The information embedded in an analogue signal therefore is always built into some constantly varying value which can be measured. By measuring it we extract the information.

The simplest example is the old fashioned wristwatch. When we glance down at its face we see hands sweeping across the dial at various speeds. They move continuously of course, covering every part of the dial at some stage of their circular journey. We judge the time of the day by the relative positions of the hands against the scale of hours, minutes and seconds printed on the watch face. This kind of information display is typically analogue. We read the message of our watch by looking at a constantly changing display. There are no gaps in the information. It is a continuous flow.

A fundamentally different kind of information is called 'digital information'. The word itself may actually be more familiar simply because it is often used to describe computers. This is an important association. Digital information is the basic language of computers.

Many years ago early efforts with electronic computers did involve some analogue devices. These involved using special circuits which performed numerical operations on electrical currents applied to them. For example, apply a current of a known size to a circuit and at the other end the current, when measured, has a value which is one half of the original. The circuit therefore is a means of dividing a number by two. However, the values measured are currents of fluctuating electrical energy. The magnitude we associate with any current is a kind of average of the fluctuation. So analogue computing was both imprecise and laborious.

You can best imagine digital information as a stream of discrete packets. Think of receiving a written message letter by letter. Individually each letter does not mean much. But the overall assembly of correctly sequenced letters into words, sentences and paragraphs, gives the meaning of the message. Each letter is a packet of information. But only all the 'information packets' in the right order give meaning to the information. If some are wrong, either because they are the wrong letters such as an occasional 'l' instead of an 'i', the message is corrupted. But it may still be understandable. It depends on the kind of message and how densely the significant information is packed into it. For example, a pleasant rambling account of a holiday in the countryside will have a good deal of flab in it. You can miss the odd word and still retain the sense. A technical message giving the specification for a new computer is much tighter. Miss a word or a number and the meaning in the message may be disastrously misinterpreted.

These ideas of discrete packets of data and the varying levels of corruptibility in messages conveyed by them are central to the world of digital information.

If we return briefly to our wristwatch, we can extend the idea of digital communication by contrasting an analogue watch with a digital one. In a digital watch we have an absolutely exact measure of time. It may be inaccurate but it is at least always exact. For example, you can always tell someone who is using a digital watch. Ask them the time and they will invariably say something like, '. . . it's 3.47'. How often do you want to know the time to the very minute? An analogue watch user will just glance at the timepiece and say, '. . . it's about a quarter to four'. In digital time-keeping it is always one time or another. It is never 'about' anything. The only instant when the digital watch is speechless is when the display flashes from one second to the next and is momentarily blank. There is a tiny gap between the flow of information packets. So it is in fact a discontinuous display.

Digital information exists only as two states while analogue deals in an infinite, continuous state. In the digital world, things are there or not there, 'on' or 'off'. There are no in-betweens. This is the reason why computers talk a language called 'binary code'. It only consists of two symbols, the numbers 1 and 0. Everything a computer does, it does in this starkly simple language of 1 and 0. Significance in the information it handles is created by placing these two symbols in different orders. In other words, the sequence 0110 means something different from 0101. A rich and powerful language is built up in this way.

The really important idea about digital information is that it is like an ordinary written message but stripped of every ounce of flab. Digital information only conveys what is significant and nothing else. Between two bits of significant information there is nothing but silence. This means that digital information can be extremely condensed on whatever medium carries it. It also tends to be clean information with no spurious 'noise'.

Now let us return quickly to the video disc. As we saw, the information carried on it is detected by measuring the lengths of pitted surfaces in each of its 54,000 tracks. There is a fluctuation between reflective and non-reflective surfaces. In other words, the information encoded on a video disc is analogue information. This makes good sense since current video technology is analogue.

However, using the same basic process as we use to make a video disc, we can encode information digitally instead. The only real difference is that we make all the pits in the disc's surface the same size. Then, as the laser beam sweeps over the surface, we only require it to detect either the presence or absence of a pit. We are no longer interested in how much pit is there; just whether it is there at all. This constant stream of information saying 'pit' or 'no pit' is of course the language of digital technology: 'on' or 'off', '1' or '0'.

If we are now concerned not with varying pit lengths but with whether a pit is there or not, we can make all the pits very small. This means we could cram a huge amount of digital data on our 12 inch disc. In practice, hybrid video discs, carrying a mixture of video and digital data, do not use quite the same encoding system. But, theoretically, a disc could hold several gigabytes of information.

One gigabyte is a thousand million bytes and, for convenience, you can imagine a byte as the information needed to print a single character like a letter or a number. Clearly, a digital disc of video disc proportions could store not just a few books but the content of a few libraries!

In practice, however, the idea of digital data stored on an optical disc takes us out of the video disc arena and into the world of compact discs.

Compact discs

Compared to video discs, compact discs were latecomers to the market. Optical video discs were first demonstrated in 1973. They became commercially available in the United States in 1978. Compact discs were not demonstrated until 1980 and did not reach the market until 1983. In the few years following the launch of compact discs, sales have outstripped video discs nearly a thousand-fold.

What is a compact disc or CD? Usually the term refers to a disc carrying digital audio. But sometimes, to distinguish them from the other uses to which CDs are being put, audio discs are called CD-As (compact discs audio). In this guide we will always refer explicitly to compact disc audio to distinguish it from other CD applications. When the term 'compact disc' is used without qualification, it will be used as a generic term.

We have in fact more or less described a compact disc. The digital optical disc outlined in the paragraphs above, is the essence of the compact disc. But, apart from the fact that (unlike video discs) compact discs carry digital information, they are also a different size. Instead of a 12-inch double-sided disc, compact discs are single-sided with a diameter of 12 centimetres (4.72 inches). They are made of a polycarbonate plastic 1.2 millimetres thick. The spiral tracks are packed to within 1.6 millionths of a metre of one another and in all are about three miles long!

Physically, they look like diminutive counterparts of the video disc. Their hardy, reflective surface gives audio compact discs a beauty that is matched by the incomparable quality of the digital sound recorded on them. Usually the music is itself first digitally recorded onto magnetic tape or disc although sometimes older analogue recordings are converted to digital. Once encoded on the compact disc, the data is read by the laser stylus as a stream of 'bits', each being pulled off the disc in less than a quarter of a millionth of a second. This rapid flow of data is passed through a digital-to-analogue converter which creates an electrical signal that can be amplified and played through a standard consumer hi-fi music system.

Unlike video discs, audio compact discs have only one kind of playback. In order to maximise playback time, Constant Linear Velocity (CLV) is the standard. The speed of the disc in fact varies from 200 to 430 rpm, depending on the position of the laser stylus. Because of this, a particular piece of music on the disc is not located by a track number but by its position on a spiral track counted in terms of the time it takes to reach it while playing back normally. This retrieval process is slower than the facility offered by Constant Angular Velocity (CAV) where searchable locations can each be ascribed an electronic marker or address. In the world of audio compact discs this is not a limitation that matters to most users. However, when we are storing other kinds of data on a compact disc, access speed becomes a serious issue.

An important feature of all compact discs is the systems built in for detecting and correcting errors in the bits of information pulled off them by the disc player. These systems, vital in any digital system, affect the way in which the data can be stored on the disc.

The degree of error detection you need depends on how densely the significant information is packed. If we return briefly to our written message from a friend, you can see that his description of a holiday in the country might include a good deal of information that could be lost without the sense of the message being affected. Music is similarly tolerant. A few lost bits of data from a Beethoven piano sonata will not be noticed even by the most acute listener. So error detection in an audio disc can be at a relatively modest level. However, if the disc is being used to store textual data digitally, later to be reconstructed on a screen by a computer, one uncorrected error bit could put an unwanted zero on the end of a crucial number. Worse still, it could be the difference between a plus and minus sign in front of your bank balance!

For CD-ROM applications the issue of error detection and correction is vital. So to support these demanding applications, systems of detection have been devised that more or less reach the limits of the possible. And, of course, if it is no longer possible for you to detect an error you certainly cannot put it right. Compact disc audio uses a detection and correction system called 'Cross-Interleaved Reed-Solomon Code' (CIRC). CD-ROM takes CIRC just as a starting point. The result is an uncorrectable error rate of one bit in ten raised to the power of twelve. This means that only one uncorrectable error will occur in a million million bits or the equivalent of about 2000 discs.

Recordable optical discs

People familiar with magnetic recording media such as audio or video tape or the floppy discs used with personal computers will notice an apparent major limitation in digital optical disc technology. The discs are read-only systems. In magnetic media it is simple to record over existing information and use the same tape or disc many times. But the technology of writing on digital optical discs is far more complex. The technology of erasing existing information and writing new material over it, is more complex still.

Systems allowing users to write to an optical disc do exist. Commonly referred to as WORMs (Write Once Read Many), these systems rely on the fact that the capacity of a disc is so huge, few people have enough data to record to fill it. Users continue to record sections of data onto the disc over a period of months or even years, until the disc is full. But it is not possible to over-write data onto an already written section or to erase anything once recorded.

Erasable discs are still some way off although prototypes already exist. However, commercial systems are not expected much before the early 1990s.

In practice, WORM systems and erasable systems are likely always to remain costly, ideal for specific, major corporate applications. They are unlikely to affect substantially the generic publishing possibilities of the disc medium where read-only systems offer all that can reasonably be required from an information product.

3

CD-ROMs: an Introduction

We now need to move away from optical disc generalities and focus attention on the CD-ROM itself. What is meant by a CD-ROM and what are the key issues surrounding its development and use?

The compact disc bonanza

Compact disc audio has been the most successful consumer electronics product since the television and it has caught on much more quickly.

In 1983 when the first players were brought to the market, sales worldwide topped 350,000. By the end of 1984 the figure was touching 1.25 million. The British Phonographic Industry reports that in 1986 player sales reached 6 million units in Britain alone. Worldwide the figure is estimated at around 14 million. This astonishing success is of course matched by sales of discs. US market researchers, Link Resources, report worldwide disc sales in 1986 of about 100 million and predict that in the United States alone, over 300 million discs will be sold in 1990. Even these huge figures are regarded by industry pundits as just the leading edge of a long-term sales penetration.

A key reason why compact disc audio has been an instant and dramatic success is that any disc will play on any player anywhere in the world. There are none of the incompatibilities that dog the computer industry. This remarkable concord was achieved by the leading developers of the technology, Philips and Sony, negotiating a set standard before the first commercial players were launched. The standard is described in a joint Philips/Sony publication called

The Red Book and is available to anyone with a licence to manufacture either discs or drives.

But issues of standardisation are simple when all you are playing back is music. The problems to be resolved are largely ones of physical compatibility in the hardware. The difficulties really begin mushrooming when the same effort to standardise as went into *The Red Book* is applied to CDs holding computer data files. However, whatever the additional standardisation issues, the use of compact discs for data storage other than music still has a big built-in advantage. Evolving from a well-established technology, mass-market sales volumes ensure economies in the manufacture of the more specialised disc drives needed and in the mastering and replication of the discs.

What is a CD-ROM?

While video disc technology was struggling to be born, a number of companies active in the information handling industry attempted to create hybrid video discs that held both analogue and digital data. Some were relatively successful in specialised applications. Perhaps the boldest effort so far, has come from the British Broadcasting Corporation's Domesday Project. Here two video discs were produced, playable only on a dedicated hardware system consisting of a computer, video disc player and a monitor. The discs are the twentieth-century equivalent of the famous survey of Britain commanded by William the Conqueror in 1086. They impressively combine over 300 megabytes of digital information with thousands of frames of analogue video. Sadly, the cost of the replay system is so high, the Domesday Project looks destined to become a commercial flop. Most other hybrid developments also suffer from the expensive, non-standard playback systems they require.

Not surprisingly therefore, the same kind of companies, together with hardware and software suppliers and publishers, became quickly interested in a digital optical disc that was fast becoming a phenomenal success in worldwide consumer markets. Here was an obvious chance to create big database information products without the problems of costly hardware configurations. All that was needed was to connect a compact disc player to a microcomputer and provide the right bit of software to run the thing. Perhaps it would even be possible to foresee a disc player with a switch on the back to transform it in an instant from an audio player to a CD-ROM player.

Of course life is never quite that simple. Despite the strong similarities between audio compact disc technology and the CD-ROM concept, the differences are important ones.

To start with, we should look at the similarities. There are two obvious ones. First, both deal with the recording, storage and retrieval of digital information. Second, both use the same physical medium of a laser-read disc, 12 centimetres in diameter. The important point about this is that these two basic similarities immediately imply a level of worldwide standardisation. At this level of the technology, where we are principally concerned with physical characteristics, the Philips/Sony Red Book type of standard applies. In fact, the extended standard for CD-ROMs takes account, in particular, of the data processing environment in which they will most commonly be used and is contained in a Philips/Sony publication known as *The Yellow Book*. However, this is just a starting point. From here on, the differences between CD audio and CD-ROM start piling up and the standards issue, in particular, becomes an especially complex problem.

Before plunging in, however, we should just briefly ensure we understand what a CD-ROM does. We have seen that physically it is much like a CD audio disc. The same silvered disc carries the same kind of spiral tracks with the same kind of microscopically pitted surface. All discs are 1.2 millimetres thick and have a hole in the middle 15 millimetres across. These likenesses also mean that CD-ROM plays back like an audio disc in the mode called Constant Linear Velocity (CLV). We have already seen that CLV maximises a laser disc's playing time. This is obviously just what people want from an audio disc. However, CLV also means that the drive must spin the disc at different speeds depending on where the data being accessed is located. This process of slowing down or accelerating the disc takes time and the speed of randomly accessing information from the disc is significantly less than under Constant Angular Velocity (CAV). This is no problem to the music lover but is an important limitation to CD-ROM users who are acutely concerned about how long it takes to find one word among millions in a huge CD database.

It is useful to have some idea of the differences in search times. Compared to a standard fixed magnetic disc drive such as a

Winchester or similar, CD-ROM search times are of the order of ten times longer. Typically, this means between a half and a full second to search from a full CD-ROM database. This may not seem very long but users who are making extensive and often complex searches will compare performance with the best offered by conventional magnetic media. Against this yardstick, CD-ROM could look very laggardly indeed. So the problem of search times is a serious drawback for CD-ROMs and emphasises why it is crucial to design the data on them with special file and index structures so that search and retrieval times are kept to an absolute minimum. With a little ingenuity, it is also possible to group large blocks of related data so anticipating likely areas of search and helping to bring down search times still further.

Obviously, the key difference between audio CDs and CD-ROM lies in the content of the data each holds. CD audio discs store nothing but audio information. CD-ROM can contain audio (and some CD-ROM products do) but typically stores textual data that can be accessed and interpreted by a computer. Used in this fashion the compact disc offers a formidable storage capacity. In terms of raw data, a single disc can hold about 600 megabytes, the equivalent of about a quarter of a million printed pages of text. In practice, a substantial part of the disc has to be occupied by indexing data and other utilities. This reduces the actual database product size to around 350 megabytes. Still huge by any standards.

In some ways the CD-ROM itself is a very straightforward addition to a computer system. A specialised disc drive is physically linked to a suitable microcomputer. Two kinds of software are then loaded into the computer. One is the device driver software that gives the computer the protocols needed so that it can have a dialogue with the drive. The other is the search and retrieval software which enables the user to locate and access information from the CD-ROM. Seen this way, the CD-ROM drive is just another computer peripheral like a floppy disc drive while the disc is just another storage device. There are two key differences. First, you cannot write data on a CD-ROM. You can only read data from it. Second, a single CD-ROM can hold as much data as about 1500 ordinary floppy discs.

So far we have emphasised the CD-ROM's capacity for storing text. Indeed manufacturers such as Philips go to some trouble to discourage people from thinking along other lines. Their view is that CD-ROM originators should use the medium for what it is best at doing. Any talk of incorporating graphics, in particular, meets with a cool response. There is obviously some sense in making CD-ROM do what it does best. But the fact remains that so far it has been the manufacturers who have told us what this is. The originators, on the whole, have done what they are told. Organisations such as Philips have their own good reasons for maintaining a narrow view of CD-ROM's future horizons. They are anxious that people do not stray from emerging *de facto* CD-ROM standards (such as the HSG proposal *see* pages 30–2) which deal principally with textual information: they fear that any exploration of new areas could plunge these fragile agreements, just now being reached, into chaos. They are also concerned to prevent hybrid uses of CD-ROM overshadowing a new evolutionary stage in compact disc technology. The development they are protecting is CD-I which stands for 'Compact Disc Interactive'. In fact, there is no need to be protective about CD-I. Its own special strengths will ensure a perfectly happy future. We will return to CD-I in more detail later, especially since it may have some important influences on fledgling CD-ROM markets.

However, the time has come when the pioneers are beginning to make their mark. Innovative publishers are beginning to push back the limits of what CD-ROMs are assumed to do best. Their message is coming across loud and clear. CD-ROM is not just a text environment. It can handle graphics and, if you want it, digitally recorded sound too. One of the best current examples of graphics handling comes from a US company called DeLorme Mapping Systems. They have created a demonstration CD-ROM world atlas with a spectacular 'zoom' feature. The user starts with a view of the whole world and can then zoom in to locate countries, then districts, then towns and even, on the ultimate level of the zoom, streets and houses. The disc features political boundaries, road systems, rivers, lakes and seas and even has a few three-dimensional displays; chiefly land elevations and ocean depths. Another US Company, Geovision, has also produced a CD-ROM map disc. This provides detailed maps of the United States at national, regional, state and metropolitan levels.

At a more popular level, US book publishers, Facts on File, have announced and demonstrated work on a major visual dictionary on CD-ROM. Best known for mass-market consumer-orientated reference publishing, Facts on File, clearly anticipate major CD-ROM markets in homes and schools. Their dictionary incorporates a good many words as well as pictures. But what is particularly striking is that some of the words are actually spoken. For example, there is a picture of a bicycle with key parts labelled in English. Using an electronic pointer such as a mouse, the user can select one of the labelled parts and hear the word translated into other languages.

So it appears that CD-ROM can do almost anything with the right technical brains behind it. Until recently there was one major limitation accepted by everyone that knew anything about the medium. CD-ROM could not handle video images very well. Full motion video at 30 frames a second was totally impossible. The problem lies in the density of data in a single frame of video. Just one frame requires about 600 kilobytes of data. So one second of full motion video means transferring 18 million bytes of data from the storage medium to the display system and doing it in just one second. The sheer volume of data needed to build a lengthy video sequence would be difficult to store, even given a CD-ROM's prodigous capacity. But leaving this aside, there is no known means of transferring digital data at the rate of 18 megabytes per second.

However, as if to prove how ill-advised it is ever to use the word 'impossible' about a technological problem, RCA has stunned experts with a technique allowing an hour of full motion digital video on a single CD-ROM. They call the system 'Digital Video Interactive' (DVI). What RCA appear to have done is invent a chip which compresses the data needed to construct the images, decompressing it when the time comes to display the video. The extent of the compression is dramatic. The 18 megabytes per second needed for full motion is cut to about 150 kilobytes, a factor of better than one hundred to one. Though the development was only announced in March 1987, RCA estimate that a commercial prototype chip will be available at the end of 1987 at a price in the order of thousands of dollars. By about 1990, however, DVI technology ought to be cheap enough to reach most current CD-ROM applications and even, perhaps, the home market.

But more important than wrangles about what a CD-ROM can or cannot handle, is the issue of hardware standards. Plenty of remarkable things are possible beyond just text handling but you need special display architecture in the hardware in order to enjoy their benefits. Sophisticated graphics on the CD-ROM can only be interpreted by microcomputers with appropriate graphics cards. Even then advanced graphics techniques will demand monitor screens of specially high resolution. The message to generic publishers is clear. Yes, you can make a CD-ROM with many spectacular features but you will probably need to sell a dedicated work station with your disc so that customers can use it. This is like having to sell an extra and costly set of eyes with a book just so people can read it. Most publishers would reject out of hand the idea of having to sell hardware to make their product useable and most would be right to do so. However, embryonic market places sometimes call for unusual sales strategies and if the CD-ROM product is of sufficiently high value, there may be an argument for selling the hardware to use it.

The important point is that once you try to push CD-ROM beyond text-handling applications, you move away from the safety of standard and commonplace hardware. It can be done but most of us would reckon that the sensible course in an already risky new area of publishing is to stay with the mainstream even if it appears to limit the kind of product you can offer.

CD-ROM standards

Traditionally, standards evolve in one of two ways. The most democratic is the standard chosen by the market place. For example, a manufacturer makes a product of a particular kind, say a video recorder, which becomes a huge success, selling in millions worldwide. The sheer dominance of the product establishes it as a *de facto* standard. This happened, for example, when the Victor Company of Japan began selling VHS video recorders in the consumer market in competition with Sony's Betamax system. Very quickly VHS became a world standard for the consumer market while Sony's system became a *de facto* standard in professional markets. The same process has taken place at least twice in the world of microcomputers. First with Digital Research's CP/M operating system and then, more recently, with the phenomenal impact of the IBM PC and the operating system, MS-DOS.

The other way standards emerge is through groups of organisations with axes to grind, coming to agreements either just before or, more commonly, soon after products are launched. Logically, the second method should serve everyone's interests best. After all, with experts on the technology talking to experts on the market, standards that are good for both the business investors and for end users should ultimately emerge. The big drawback is that the process can be very long-winded. Sometimes, in the time that it takes, *de facto* standards overtake the deliberations of the experts.

While there is still some danger of this happening as far as CD-ROM is concerned, discussions on standards have made remarkably swift progress. Philips and Sony, the main compact disc proponents, gave the lead by establishing *The Yellow Book* standard. We have already touched on this and outlined its role as a physical specification of the CD-ROM medium. A key principle of *The Yellow Book* is its insistence on CLV playback. But it also deals with the physical dimensions of discs, recording density track layout, the way pits are arranged on the disc and the rigorous error detection and correction scheme that CD-ROM requires.

The physical standard is the bedrock on which CD-ROM development is based. However, beyond this lie more complex and contentious standardisation issues. The definition of a CD-ROM as a physical object is one thing. How you store information on it is quite another. Standardising the way data are embodied on the disc is technically described as the 'Volume and File Structure Standard'. It is more commonly referred to as the 'logical' level of CD-ROM standardisation. This difficult area is concerned with determining the best possible common structures and interrelations between volumes, files, records and directories in the database. The objective is to make sure that different operating systems running on different computers can all make sense of the information stored on any given CD-ROM. For example, if a CD-ROM drive is linked to a particular computer by a physical interface and some appropriate device driver software, the computer system sees the disc as a lot of physical sectors containing digital information. When an applications program such as some search and retrieval software is running and trying to address the disc, it sees the situation logically rather than physically. In this context, the disc is a collection of files each with its own unique name. The software has to be able to call up a particular file, open it and, no matter how long or short it is, read it.

The most energetic force in the logical standards debate has been the High Sierra Group (HSG), named after the Nevada hotel in which, late in 1985, it held its first meeting. The group consisted of a range of hardware and software specialists, all with major interests in CD-ROM development. It included such companies as Apple, DEC, Hitachi, Microsoft, Philips, Sony, Microware and 3M. IBM was asked to participate but turned down the invitation.

In the months following its inaugural meeting, HSG received contributions from three other major bodies: the Information Industry Association (the US trade group); the American Library Association; and, representing companies throughout Europe, the Optical Disc Forum. Thousands of man hours of debate and discussion culminated in 1986 in the publication of the HSG's draft standard. This is now in the hands of the US National Information Standards Organisation (NISO) and is well on its way to becoming accepted internationally. Anybody wanting to examine the technical details of the proposal or the issues which it addresses, can go to the voluminous literature that is widely available. Here, we need only understand the status and implications of the proposal.

Essentially it sets out a common volume, file and directory structure intelligible to all major computer operating systems. It seeks to optimise the performance of CD-ROMs, in particular making the best of the relatively slow search and retrieval times. Additionally it tries to avoid constraints that might restrict future innovative developments using CD-ROM.

With the standard, CD-ROM publishers should be able to produce a single version of their disc that will work on all CD-ROM drives and with any microcomputer so long as appropriate device drivers are available. Because HSG were anticipating a market in which there might be a wide range of marriages between many different makes of drive and many different computers, their standard does not embody requirements for device driver software. This means that device drivers stay the concern of the computer suppliers or the suppliers of their operating systems rather than CD-ROM publishers. If necessary the publisher could offer a variety of device drivers on a single floppy disc bundled with the search and retrieval software. Once loaded, the system could self-configure to the appropriate driver making compatibility issues transparent to the end user. The only constraint on the system, which the publisher would have to address specifically, is the operating system of the computer being used. And since MS-DOS is today the worldwide *de facto* standard, this is hardly a major headache. The only other 'version' publishers might want to take seriously is Apple's DOS. With Apple holding the giant's share of the huge and lucrative US schools computer market, it is little wonder that some CD-ROM publishers are already establishing Apple compatible software for their products.

It looks as if the HSG proposal will soon be an international standard. Its draft has already been examined by the US National Standards Organisation (NISO) and in October 1986 NISO handed over the proposals to an editorial team who will prepare the document for submission to NISO voting members for a ballot. These include the members of the European Computer Manufacturers Association. It will then be handed to the International Organisation for Standards for implementation as a formally accepted international standard.

However, even on the surprisingly swift time-scale that events are following, much remains to be done.The process is likely to take a few years even if all goes smoothly. This means that there is still plenty of time for someone to undo all the efforts of HSG and the other bodies concerned with the standardisation issue. All it takes is one organisation with sufficient muscle, innovation and resolve to go all out to create a *de facto* standard before the HSG proposals are made 'law'. Not many companies are capable of the feat but one such company is IBM who so far have remained aloof from the wrangles and debates. Some commentators are already warning the proponents of the HSG proposals to 'watch out for Big Blue!'

Search and retrieval software

Should CD-ROMs be a medium for expert information scientists or should they be easily useable by anyone who needs to find something out? Traditionally, trained librarians have been the main custodians of large databases. Information users have needed to apply to the experts to get what they want or what they think they want. Up to now this has made good sense. There is, after all, a world of difference between simply looking up the life span of a penguin in an encyclopaedia and searching for technical references to specific uses of a chemical compound buried in an entire scientific library consisting of thousands of books and journals. In the comfort of our homes or in our offices we can use the familiar skills gathered from our everyday experiences of using books and journals to get simple information from simple information sources. But extracting specific references or correlations of information from really big and complex databases requires a high level of skill. It is something that only professionals can do quickly and well.

When the first big databases went electronic in the shape of commercial on-line systems, libraries of books and journals were reduced to mainframe computer files and the tools available to dig around them were the proprietary software packages developed to search the databases and retrieve whatever was wanted from them via appropriate computer terminals. Although these kinds of facilities are today widely available through commercial on-line databases to which anyone with enough money can subscribe, the search and retrieval software is often unfriendly enough to discourage all but the professionals or the uncommonly persistent. There is a good reason for this. Most on-line vendors with numerous different databases to sell wanted a single software package that could cope with all the products. It would have been commercially impractical to consider anything else. As a result, the major mainframe packages have had to maintain such a level of generality that questions of user friendliness have taken a relatively low priority. But complex and unmemorable command structures leave most untrained users frustrated and weary of constantly leafing through the often unreadable manuals that go with the software. Far from being able to quickly locate information or even occasionally to browse for that unexpected and helpful fact or reference, the user is often left without the information he was after and bitterly contemplating the huge bill run up in the lengthy search process.

In such database delivery systems, speedy use is crucial. Most commercial on-line databases make their money out of connect times. The user pays large sums for every minute he is on-line and linked with the system. So unfriendly software is best left to those trained to use it and the monopoly of large databases by information professionals is more or less reinforced.

The situation is not quite as bad as this may sound and some search and retrieval packages do nowadays seem to be addressing the issue of user friendliness but it is clear that it will take some time to break down the notion that in general experts should moderate our access to databases.

In recent years the on-line industry has spawned a range of fast free-text retrieval systems for databases held on mainframes. Among the best-known is software from Battelle Software Products (now re-named Information Dimensions Inc), BRS and Harwell. The growth of the mini and microcomputer markets has meant that companies like these have often adapted their packages to run on these smaller machines. Now that CD-ROMs are here linked to microcomputers, it is not surprising that Battelle, BRS and others are offering their services to the fledgling CD-ROM publishing industry.

Search and retrieval software is more than a pair of hands that can sift and examine large quantities of data and return what is needed to a user. The choice of the software fundamentally influences the initial design and indexing of the database. For example, a database designed for use with Battelle's MicroBASIS cannot generally also be interrogated by BRS's package BRS/Search. In other words, from the outset, a would-be CD-ROM publisher has to work closely with one of these software vendors and plan, organise, structure and index their database product according to the vendor's specifications. This means that the choice of search software is a key decision to be made early in the publishing process.

It is also a crucial choice, one that will ultimately have a huge influence on the success of the product. We have to remember that CD-ROM users are not interested in the clever technology that has brought the data they have purchased to their computer screens. They are even less interested in the challenges of determining the best possible logical standards for the medium. What they care about is what they have bought and what they have bought is an information product, hopefully an extremely powerful one, which they want to use quickly and easily. Seen this way, the chosen search and retrieval software becomes the user's window on his database. It totally determines how the user experiences the product. There is therefore only one choice more important for the publisher: the choice of what database to put on the CD-ROM in the first place.

The future of the CD-ROM market will hinge on how quickly we understand the real significance of truly user-friendly search facilities. So far the role of on-line software vendors in the off-line industry has simply transferred the unwelcoming characteristics of on-line software packages to the first CD-ROM packages. The term 'off-line' distinguishes databases on CD-ROMs, which are discrete, physically independent products, from databases held in mainframe computers and distributed to users 'on-line' through telecommunication links. However, some off-line specific packages are now emerging and hopefully these will recognise that typical CD-ROM users do not have the same tolerance towards complicated and unwieldy search software as do the professional users of on-line databases.

Among the newcomers are Reference Technology of Boulder, Colorado who, having been around since 1982, are considered 'veterans' in their field! They have three related software products covering all that is required in CD-ROM data preparation and access. STA/File and STA/Text are the packages that provide their search and retrieval facilities. The romantically named SilverPlatter organisation with offices in Massachusetts and London, has also developed software dedicated to CD-ROMs. Time Management Software (TMS) of Stillwater, Oklahoma, has created LaserDOS which is really a utility allowing access to large volumes of data through the widely available MS-DOS operating system.

Gary Kildall who played a big part in developing the CP/M operating system for Digital Research, set up a company in Monterey, California, dedicated to the optical disc market. The company was known originally as the Activenture Corporation but has recently been renamed KnowledgeSet. Their Knowledge Retrieval System (KRS) was used with the first consumer CD-ROM product, Grolier's electronic encyclopaedia, published in the autumn of 1986. It sets a shining example of how software designed for both friendliness and search power can make access to a nine million word database a simple, quick and pleasurable experience. Grolier's Peter Cook worked closely with KnowledgeSet throughout the development of the product. Significantly, although today Cook is a respected expert on optical disc publishing, his background lies in book design and he has strong views on how things should look, whether on a page or a screen. He firmly believes that CD-ROM products must be attractive to users both on a practical and a visual level. 'My key concern', says Cook, 'is to make the system completely transparent to its users. They can forget the hardware and the software and become absorbed in the information world they are exploring. I was looking for this standard of software friendliness when I began talking to Gary Kildall.'

Whether or not KRS completely fulfills this aim of creating an almost invisible interface between the user and the data, the idea is an exciting one. The message to publishers is clear. The search and retrieval software you choose determines how your customers experience your product. Accordingly its design must be a blend of power and friendliness. It should aim to be so unobtrusive that its users forget about it altogether. On-line database vendors have never learned this lesson or, if they have, are constrained by the economics of their business to ignore it. CD-ROM publishers can and must both learn it and apply it if the off-line industry is to have a future.

CD-ROM applications

Since the first prototype CD-ROM drives were demonstrated in November 1984, the number of available disc products has grown steadily. Estimates of how many CD-ROM products exist vary wildly. Learned Information's 1986 Optical Publishing Directory lists 42 commercially available products in the United States. Mandarin Communications estimated about 70 at the end of 1986. Some commentators have claimed several hundred discs available but are probably including in-house discs for corporate use and the many prototype and trial discs that have been made in order to give would-be publishers some safe, low cost experience of the medium. The true number at the end of 1986 was probably between 70 and 80 with plausible estimates of around five times as many by the end of 1987.

Of those discs available at the end of 1986, 17 library automation products could be counted with seven companies each offering MARC records (Machine Readable Catalogue — standard machine readable code for keeping bibliographical information). About 20 or so fall into the category of library and general reference with between 30 and 40 aimed at individual end users, mainly professionals in specific fields. Curiously in such a restricted market, several publishers were offering identical databases, although with differing search software. In addition to the seven offerings of MARC records, the medical database, 'Medline' was available from three companies and the educational bibliographic database, ERIC. was also available from three.

While it serves little purpose to catalogue all the different products here, it is useful to make a brief survey of some of the more interesting releases and get some sense of the diversity that is already becoming apparent. We have already touched on a particularly interesting example, the first disc aimed at the consumer market, Grolier's *Electronic Encyclopaedia*.

The Grolier disc

Some explanation is needed as to why the disc exists at all. For all its admirable qualities, it is surely a product way ahead of its time. Indeed many would question whether there will ever be a time for consumer market CD-ROMs. Surprisingly even some of the team at Grolier can be heard expressing doubts from time to time. So why did the disc get made? The answer lies in Grolier's whole strategy towards electronic publishing. Grolier is the biggest publisher of encyclopaedias in the world and probably its single most important product is the twenty-volume *Academic American Encyclopaedia*. In spite of its name, it is not in the least academic. On the contrary it is an excellent, mainstream consumer reference product bought by thousands of households throughout the United States.

The top management of Grolier are shrewd, tough businessmen. Not the kind of people you would expect to invest in inherently unprofitable ventures such as leading edge electronic publishing. Far better, after all, to be 'trailing edge' so you can exploit the markets expensively created by the pioneers. But in the early 1980s, Grolier's main board established a separate operating company called Grolier Electronic Publishing. As if to emphasise the separateness, the new operation was located some miles from Grolier's Danbury headquarters, in downtown Manhattan.

The first major project was to convert the text of the *Academic American* into an on-line database. This task completed, Grolier began selling their product through a number of on-line vendors. While they remain coy about the commercial success of this first electronic product, there is little doubt that their sales are extremely modest. The on-line industry in general generates disappointing revenues so one can imagine the kind of response a purely consumer-orientated database would receive. The next project was a major interactive video disc encyclopaedia bringing the company into its first contact with optical disc technology. The project foundered when first its UK publishing partner, Longman, pulled out, followed soon after by the crucial partner in Japan.

Although it is hard to see how the new operation could be generating anything but thunderous losses given these reverses, another optical disc project emerged in the form of the *Academic American* on CD-ROM. It is now quite clear that Grolier was prepared to remain relaxed about its unprofitable electronic publishing adventure simply because it was not being regarded as a normal business activity. Grolier Electronic Publishing sits somewhere on its parent company's public relations budget. The Grolier bosses had appreciated that among their type of customers, a high profile in bold, exciting new technology publishing would greatly enhance their reputation for having 'the right stuff', the forward-looking spirit that made America great. In the words of Grolier's advertising: 'Welcome to Tomorrow!'. In addition there was always the chance that these embryonic, futuristic markets could come good and that one of these electronic investments might make real money.

It is even possible that the CD-ROM might already be into profit. It has sold almost 2500 units since release at a retail price of $199 and is shortly to go into a new edition at $299. This makes it the biggest CD-ROM seller ever by a very large margin. No others are likely to have topped 200 sales. The Grolier disc supports a range of drives in MS-DOS including those made by Philips, Sony and Hitachi and will shortly be available in a version suitable for Apple microcomputers. In this way Grolier expect to sell substantial quantities to US schools where Apple holds well over half of the market. Their investment in producing the disc was kept low through utilising the already electronically captured encyclopaedia in its on-line form. Also Grolier worked closely with Gary Kildall's, then recently formed, Activenture Corporation, who were keen enough for the experience and visibility offered by the Grolier project to agree an inexpensive deal. For Activenture too, the disc was a major public relations effort.

Whatever the business rationale for the project, the disc itself is an impressive piece of publishing, at least in terms of its design and presentation. Activenture (now KnowledgeSet) provided their Knowledge Retrieval System (KRS) with built-in easy to use selection of the right device driver software for the disc drive being used. Apart from a visually attractive on-screen format, KRS offers an excellent combination of powerful search and retrieval together with simplicity of use. A feature that has been emphasised by Grolier is the so-called browse mode allowing users to run through the huge database until something interesting catches their eye. This kind of approach is an exciting departure from the database philosophy that argues for specific answers to specific enquiries. It recognises that often information users do not even know what it is they want to know. Serendipity, the accidental discovery of interesting and useful information, is an important and motivating aspect of any knowledge system and something that can flourish in CD-ROM technology so long as the search and retrieval software allows it to do so.

The Microsoft Bookshelf

Less than a year after Grolier released their remarkable CD-ROM, Microsoft, originators of the MS-DOS operating system, launched their integrated CD-ROM 'reference library'. Although having clear consumer market appeal, Microsoft see their *Bookshelf* as the first low cost generic CD-ROM product for the business market. Priced at an attractive $295, the *Bookshelf* combines ten reference works on a single disc. The reference databases include Houghton Mifflin's *American Heritage Dictionary*, Bartlett's *Quotations*, Roget's *Thesaurus*, a world almanac, a spelling checker, a style manual and a directory of US zip codes.

The real power of the system lies in its close integration with any of the major word processing packages currently available. Microsoft's sales literature says, '. . . Bookshelf actually works from within your word processor. So instead of having to stop what you're doing, find the reference book you need, search through it, find the relevant information, and then copy or apply the information to your document, a few quick keystrokes get you what you're looking for quickly and easily. . . . You can use a word in your document to trigger a search in a reference source or you can enter your search criteria directly. Or you can browse through the complete reference works. . . . and Bookshelf makes it easy to copy the information you have found into your document. . . . [it] also contains a set of writing tools that can help make your writing clear, concise and letter perfect.'

Bookshelf is specifically designed to work with a dozen of the world's leading word processors but Microsoft's marketing director, Carl Stork, claims it is written to work with 'virtually all programs on the market'. The target market is very broad including anybody who generates a lot of documents. While writers and journalists are the most obvious users, many professionals in other fields are bound to be attracted by such a substantial package at such low cost. Stork comments, 'it's really the first horizontal use of CD-ROM in a personal computing environment. . . . almost all the products we've seen so far are very vertical, with the exception of Grolier's encyclopaedia'.

An interesting feature of the Bookshelf concept is its use of a multiplicity of databases as a logically integrated resource. This approach to big database products could hold real promise if it is extended into areas of professional reference. One could see powerful and unique research tools built up from a number of distinct but generically similar databases with the user moving easily among them perhaps spotting correlations which might never come to light in any other way. In this context, the individual databases could be imagined as the elements of a superdatabase offering a totally new kind of information product.

The CD-ROM atlas

The first thing to know about the CD-ROM atlas is that it does not really exist. At the time of writing it remains one of the many prototypes developed both to test the medium and to demonstrate possible applications to potential customers by showing them something concrete. We have already briefly mentioned mapping applications of CD-ROM when we considered whether it could ever truly be a medium for graphics. The most important and interesting development is the one from DeLorme Mapping Systems of Freeport, Maine.

The disc they have so far demonstrated is designed to illustrate the capability of CD-ROM in handling digitised maps. The main points they seek to make to organisations familiar with the conventional heavy hardware of such a system, are that the database is easy to use and that the hardware is low cost and relatively portable. The first version of the 'atlas' incorporates political boundaries, towns and cities, major roads, rivers, lakes, land elevations and sea and ocean depths. For most of the maps, the scale is about twenty miles to the inch but some sample areas have been included at one inch to 400 feet.

An appealing feature of the access software is a zoom effect that enables the user to 'fly' into an area of interest. Once the system is turned on, the first screen shows an image of the whole world. The user then selects a region of interest with the on-screen cursor and selects the zoom function to move down for a more detailed look. Once the area of interest is enlarged, further zooms can be made.

Each time, the cursor position defines the centre of the map display so the user can adjust the location laterally between zooms by repositioning the cursor. So far, DeLorme can offer sixteen consecutive levels of zoom. The scale halves with each level so the amount of detail increases fourfold. If the appropriate database of mapping information was available on the disc, the zoom system would ultimately focus on an area just a half a mile square. DeLorme have not yet implemented this level of detail. An alternative means of accessing the database is by selecting latitude and longitude together with a required map scale.

While there is nothing new about digitised maps, the CD-ROM approach is the first to offer the potential of a worldwide system available on low-cost, portable hardware. For the first time, the benefits of digital mapping could become available to anyone. Perhaps the most obvious of these is the ease with which digital maps can be kept up-to-date or enhanced with additional information. Also there is the possibility that with the right kind of applications software, users will be able to manipulate the maps to explore the implications of changing land use and to see the three-dimensional realities behind the two-dimensional displays. There is a wealth of possibilities.

The range of possible applications even for the existing type of system is enormous. In a ship or an aircraft the CD-ROM could be linked to on-board navigation equipment so that the vehicle's position could be constantly displayed on the map display. In military applications, rapid assessments of geographical factors could be made, speeding up the whole process of tactical decision making. Any business with mobile and dispersed operations could benefit from the system. Whether or not DeLorme's 'World Atlas' gets beyond the demonstration stage, their work to date suggests how powerfully CD-ROM can be adapted to a graphics-based environment.

Two basic points need emphasis, however, before we become too intoxicated by the idea. First, the demonstration only manipulates a restricted database. Covering the whole world or even individual continents adequately means a vastly enlarged database certainly spanning several discs. This is bound to restrict the user's freedom and might substantially undermine certain kinds of application. Additionally, DeLorme would need to convince potential users that speed and flexibility of access would remain substantially unaffected by greatly enlarging the database. Second, the system's ability to handle graphics is of course strongly dependent on the display architecture of the hardware. A computer and monitor available and used by an organisation for other purposes will almost certainly be inadequate. This means that a dedicated work station may be needed. This will be of little significance to users who have major, high-value applications in mind but will certainly deter users to whom the value of digitised maps is somewhat marginal.

The business database

An obvious applications area for CD-ROM is business data. There are two good reasons for this. First, access to the right business data can be the difference between good and bad corporate decisions. This can mean the difference between making and losing large sums of money. So access to the data can be very valuable indeed. Second, the potential users have the money to buy the appropriately highly priced information product. Up to now, this market, thirsty for timely and comprehensive corporate and financial information, has been addressed mainly by the on-line industry. CD-ROM offers a real challenge with much lower costs than on-line counterparts and the convenience of desktop availability at any moment of the day. Indeed without the burden of connect times to pay for, users can have their CD-ROM database switched on all the time.

Some of the first people to see the alternative attraction of CD-ROM have been on-line vendors themselves. In January 1986, The Disclosure Information Group, well known in the United States for their on-line business databases, announced *Compact Disclosure*, their first CD-ROM product. It is effectively an off-line version of 'Disclosure Online', a database of companies whose shares are traded on American stock exchanges. On a single disc, *Compact Disclosure* gives detailed financial and business information on more than 10,000 public companies registered with the US Securities and Exchange Commission. Each entry in the database is built up from publicly available facts and figures drawn from such sources as company financial returns, registration documents and reports to shareholders. Disclosure provides about 300 lines or 20,000 characters of information. Numerical data includes balance sheets going back two or three financial years, profit and loss statements for the last three years and quarterly results since the end of the last financial year. Qualitative information includes details of the companies' directors or officers, a complete list of subsidiary companies and excerpts from the most recent annual reports to the shareholders.

The search and retrieval software which runs only under MS-DOS is a close derivative of on-line packages. Two types are available. One, called 'Easy Menu Mode', is aimed at beginners. It resembles MicroDisclosure, a menu-driven search package designed to make searching Disclosure's on-line database easy for novice users. Although there is some trade-off between power and ease of use, the menu-driven option is still capable of quite elaborate searches. These do take much longer however than the mode designed for experienced database users. This is a command-driven system which emulates a powerful on-line search package called 'Dialog II'. If users are already familiar with the Dialog on-line database which hosts Disclosure and which employs the package, they will be able to use *Compact Disclosure* in this most powerful mode without difficulty. The uninitiated, however, will find it complex and difficult to learn.

Disclosure offer their CD-ROM in a number of price options. Every one, however, includes a Philips CD-ROM drive together with an interface for an IBM or IBM compatible microcomputer. The drive becomes the subscriber's after two years. At the time of writing, the full corporate charge including quarterly updates is $4500 per year with a $1000 discount if the updates are waived. The educational and library discount is $1300 dollars. A further small discount is available if the purchaser does not want the disc drive. So the product is far from cheap. Certainly a dramatic contrast to the Grolier encyclopaedia or Microsoft's *Bookshelf*, even if these particular products do not include the cost of a drive. However, *Compact Disclosure* may look interesting to on-line users who are paying $90 for every hour of time spent searching both financial and management data.

While it is not surprising to see organisations like Disclosure exploring new avenues in database products, it is perhaps difficult to understand their overall strategy. Either they hope that *Compact Disclosure* is an added value product which will bring them revenues they would not otherwise expect to get, or they are weaning their on-line customers away from Dialog and reassigning them to a product which Disclosure controls directly without the need for a host.

An applications explosion?

We have touched briefly on the growing diversity of CD-ROM products emerging from the information industry. Whether or not economic markets exist for these and the many other CD-ROMs now appearing, there is a remarkable energy at work among publishers. Some argue that this energy could well be the spark that touches off the tinderbox. Even if a single database, while interesting enough in itself, is insufficient to encourage end users to take the plunge, the availability of increasing numbers of such databases could just convince them. Philips themselves have always maintained that CD-ROM is suitable for relatively small niche markets. So long as the right database is matched to the right niche, the argument goes, a CD-ROM will make money. The real problem, however, is knowing what is the right database and the right niche. So far, for all their energy, many publishers are failing to make the match.

Recently Learned Information's newsletter *Monitor* contained the headline, 'At last, a *sensible* CD-ROM product'. They were referring to the British Post Office's CD-ROM of the 23.5 million postcodes which identify the 23.5 million individual homes and businesses in the UK. An inverted index is used to enable users to get any British address complete with full postcode from partial information. Worst access time is said to be about two seconds. Leaving aside the merits or drawbacks of this particular product, the point that *Monitor* was emphasising with its rather unkind headline was that too few CD-ROMs appearing today have really been thought through by their publishers. The variety of products queuing up for their niche markets may still get a very cool reception from the paying public. The on-line database industry has spent twenty years paying for its publishing mistakes. Perhaps the explosion of CD-ROM applications now taking place is just a sign that the off-line industry is about to begin doing the same thing.

4

On-line or Off-line Databases?

This is not a book about on-line databases. Neither is it a book seeking to manufacture a contest between on-line and off-line database industries. There is, however, a largely misdirected debate emerging which makes an issue out of whether one form of database provision is superior to the other. On-line database vendors are becoming defensive while CD-ROM proponents are growing shrill. Certainly some important cross-links between the two types of provision exist but sometimes listening to the arguments is like watching two fencers fight without their foils ever touching. To have a balanced view of CD-ROM, therefore, we need to consider some of the characteristics of both types of database to see where they compare, where they contrast and how, commercially, they relate to one another. To do this, we have to start by examining the background and record of the on-line industry. First, however, let us be clear about the basic elements of an on-line database.

Characteristics of on-line provision

What is an on-line database system? The three key elements are a store of information in machine-readable form (the database), a mainframe computer with communications facilities (the host computer) and someone with an appropriate computer terminal and telecommunications links so that information can be transferred back and forth between the terminal and the host (the customer). Those who provide the substance of the database are called 'information providers' while those running the big computer systems are termed 'hosts'. Customers are often 'end users'.

Often the database originates from one or more printed works. Frequently it is a bibliographic record of books, journals and articles in one or more specific subject areas. The content and type of database obviously varies widely. However, it is common either for the host to acquire a licence from the original publisher in return for some kind of royalty or for the host to assist the publisher to mount the database and so make it available to customers. In this case, the publisher gets most of the resulting revenues and pays the host for mounting and updating the database product and for storing and maintaining it in the host computer.

For a print-based publisher, on-line opportunities can look like some purely added value business. Nowadays, most books and journals are held in machine-readable form for typesetting purposes, usually on magnetic tape. It is tempting to imagine simply plugging such a tape directly into a host computer's memory banks and so create an on-line product from a print product quickly and at negligible cost. Unfortunately the reality is not so straightforward. Usually publishers' tapes contain embedded typesetting codes which control the typographic design and layout of the printed page. These generally have to be stripped out before it is possible to mount the data on an existing on-line system. In addition to the problem of embedded extraneous codes there is the issue of database structure. While the fields and records of a book's machine-readable database may be appropriate to the book as the ultimate information product, it may not have either the rigour, or the detailed subdivisional structure, needed for a satisfactory on-line offering. Finally, the particular search and retrieval software used by a particular host may have complex structural implications too.

In simplest terms, print publishers cannot mount their products on-line without a good deal of time, trouble, money and technical know-how. However, it is sometimes possible to find on-line hosts so keen to acquire a particular print-based property to add to their clutch of databases, that they are prepared to shoulder all the problems themselves. In this case, the publisher can regard the on-line arrangements in the same way as any other subsidiary rights deal. It generates some welcome revenue unencumbered by a manufacturing cost or overheads and, so long as the publisher is satisfied that the copyright of the licensed property will be protected from abuse, it can be an agreeable way of making the title profit and loss report look slightly more rosy. What this type of arrangement fails to do is to introduce print publishers to on-line publishing. They remain as ignorant of the issues involved as they do of the film industry when they sell the movie rights to a new novel.

The details of marketing on-line products are complex and difficult to generalise about, but usually customers subscribe to a service, paying a certain amount for access to one or more database products. Thereafter, they are charged a fee for the time they are connected on-line. Since a part of this time is taken up in setting the parameters of their search, it is as well for customers to plan their search before they are connected to the system, so that they can go in and out quickly. Obviously a key factor in this is the friendliness of the search and retrieval software on a particular system. If users have to spend time just mastering command structures and protocols, the connect-time bills are going to become infuriatingly large even before any information has been gleaned.

Today systems known as 'gateways' have introduced a new freedom for on-line customers who by subscribing to one service gain access through gateways to many others. By late 1986 nearly a third of all public databases were accessible via gateways of different kinds. The easiest type to use is based on the EasyNet model, pioneered in 1982 by Telebase Systems of Pennsylvania. This is really an intelligent interface between the non-expert customer and a variety of different databases mounted on different host computers. Using a menu-driven question and answer system, EasyNet determines in which of the many databases it can address lies the information that the customer is after. Then it connects to the appropriate host computer, asks the appropriate questions of the database and provides the customer with the answer. There are many legal, technical and commercial problems plaguing gateway development. But it is already clear that on-line customers like them and this is enough to suggest that their numbers will continue to grow.

On-line: the story so far

Nearly twenty years of the on-line industry proves that there is nothing new about database publishing. In a general sense, of course, book publishers with lists of reference materials have been in the database business for many years before on-line vendors ever appeared. But when the first public on-line systems emerged, there was a real belief that computer technology would offer something radically new and would revolutionise the provision of reference data to professional, academic, business and even domestic users. Indeed the model looked exciting. A huge amount of textual data could be held in a central mainframe computer while users many miles, even continents, away could link their own terminals to the computer by means of a telephone call and an appropriate modem, to enable the exchange of digital information via the telephone line. Then, using powerful search and retrieval software made available by the database vendor, the user could make intricate searches of the huge body of available information to get the answers needed. The database was potentially impressive both in terms of its sheer volume and in the way in which it could be kept up to date, virtually on a minute by minute basis, by the database vendor. In retrospect we can easily see why the first on-line pioneers were optimistic about the medium and its future.

The reality has been a story of disappointment and failure. Today, nearly twenty years on, there are about 3200 commercial on-line databases worldwide held by around 500 hosts. About twenty of these account for 80 per cent of all on-line usage. Among all the untold gigabytes of stored information, there is little that actually finds a significant market. Indeed the total number of on-line users is under 100,000. The on-line industry has built itself a data mountain that no-one wants.

The small growth in the market over the years reflects the industry's failure to come up with the right products. Worldwide the market today is probably worth about $350 million. Some 70 per cent of the turnover is generated in the United States. Apart from a few 'giants' such as Dialog and Mead Data Central, most on-line vendors have businesses worth less than $10 million, with a large number well under $5 million. With the inevitably high operating costs of this kind of business, it is hard to see how any can be making a profit. Indeed, the whole question of industry turnover and profitability is a delicate issue. People in the business either become very shy or very defensive when money is mentioned. It is as if there is a huge underlying embarrassment that, after so much time, talk, effort and ballyhoo, the whole industry adds up to so little. No-one wants to admit that on-line is not working, that its history is one of failure rather than achievement and that, if it ever really knew where it was going, it certainly does not know any longer. Because of this, it is hard to get believeable figures. Commonsense and everything one can glean from the market place suggests that few if any vendors are making real money from their databases. In a London database forum recently, Jim Ducker, doyen of the UK industry, claimed that not even Dialog was in profit. He suggested that the only two profitable vendors were probably Mead and Dow Jones. It hardly matters whether Ducker is right or wrong. The main point is that the answer lies in these sorts of numbers. There may be one or two vendors that are making money from on-line. Perhaps there are even three or four. How many exactly or who they are matters less than the fact that they are so few. After twenty years and over 3000 database products, we are left with a small, unprofitable industry which appears to have lost its way. If on-line provision disappeared overnight, the sad fact is that few information users would notice and still fewer would mourn its passing.

The database product

Where did the on-line industry go wrong? In simplest terms, it failed to give information users what they want. In fact the industry's mistake, compounded time and again over the years, has been to start with a product and look for a market. Of course, the issues are not as simple as determining what information people need just in terms of its content. Naturally this is very important but on-line provision is less about content than it is about design and delivery. When we use the word 'product' in an on-line context we mean a package of features, each of which is a key issue in itself. The editorial concept of the content of the database is just one of those features.

The other features comprising the database product — and this is true in both on or off-line scenarios — have less to do with what the information is than how it is used. In examining CD-ROM systems, we have already touched upon the vital part played by search and retrieval software. It needs emphasis time and again that the way users perceive the database product is crucially determined by this software. It defines the product as much as the content does, possibly more. Of course, it is a simplification to focus upon the software alone. The internal structuring and indexing of the database will affect the way in which the software performs and such inner design considerations are a key aspect in determining the power of the product. What this really says is that a database will have value essentially through the ways in which it can be used. This raises a fundamental problem for those of us who like to start with a market before deciding on what to publish. If we define our information product strongly in terms of its manner of use, we obviously need to know how our target customers actually use information. In other words, while getting content right we may get structure and function hopelessly wrong.

The history of on-line tells us that either this has not yet been understood or on-line publishers have simply been showing a very poor grasp of how people actually want and need to use information. Judging by what is said and written, the latter seems more probable. The harsh reality is that information publishers, even those who have for generations been successfully selling their books, know surprisingly little about the real character of their markets. No doubt, good editors will know the size of the market for which they publish. They will know something about what should go inside the books they develop and a little about the production values needed to ensure a competitive product. But such editors, the lifeblood of conventional publishing operations, know astonishingly little about how their customers actually need to use information. More than this, publishers' editors can rarely generalise beyond the format and constraints of the only product they can really visualise — the book. This may sound a little hard on the many skilful and talented editors who are keeping publishers all over the world in healthy profit. In fact editorial skills are subtle and demanding and the success of the good editor should be warmly applauded. But the fact remains that they can make profitable products without understanding how their customers really use information and, probably because they do not need to know, they not only do not know but many do not know they do not know! There remains a wishful fantasy that publishers, through their editorial teams, really have some intimate knowledge of the people who use their books. None of this matters so long as publishers stick to books. When they turn to databases things can go badly wrong.

On-line characteristics

To draw any useful parallels between on-line and off-line database provision, it is helpful to crystallise the key characteristics of on-line systems. They can be crudely summarised as size, timeliness and search power.

The database in an on-line system can in principle be as large as the largest mainframe computer memory. So the on-line product can easily dwarf the most extensive print-based reference works. Mead Data Central, one of the world's largest on-line vendors, announced recently that by the end of 1986 their total database size exceeded 140 gigabytes with 30 being added in the course of that year. Their total on-line storage potential stood at an astonishing 240 gigabytes, the equivalent of around a million floppy discs full of data! Huge databases can offer a comprehensiveness in a given subject area that no other medium has so far approached and this can be a persuasive feature in areas like law and medicine, for example, where having access to all available information can be the difference between professional success and total disaster. However, size can bring its own problems. Simply because there are so few constraints on database size, the publisher, in pursuit of comprehensiveness, may allow the product to become too large. Indeed because comprehensiveness can become such an issue, on-line publishers are likely to go to extremes, including material that is unlikely ever to be accessed. This leads to unnecessarily big databases requiring users to make more elaborate and more lengthy searches to find the answers they are after. In other words, the lack of constraint on database size leads to a lack of editorial discipline in devising the product.

Not only can on-line databases be massive, they can also be kept up-to-date almost on a moment to moment basis. Of course frequent updating presupposes access to, and the capacity to process, the newly available or refreshed data. In dealing with very large information products this may prove a mammoth undertaking in itself. However, this is the vendor's problem. So far as the customer is concerned, the timeliness of information can often be the crucial factor in the value of the database. An obvious example is the business operator who takes key decisions on the basis of fast-changing financial information. In some business environments, access to up-to-the-minute statistical, price or exchange rate information can mean the difference between right and wrong decisions worth huge sums. No other medium can compete with the timeliness of on-line provision. So in certain situations there is no substitute for it.

However, size and timeliness in an on-line product amounts to little if you cannot get at the information you need, quickly and easily. The key to this, of course, is the search and retrieval software provided to database users: the basic instrument that makes sense of the whole database edifice. Without it all you have is a data mountain that few would want to climb. At its best the software is the real source of a database's power, enabling rapid and complex searches for specific items or correlations of information.

While this is not the place for any serious critique of search and retrieval software, it is worth emphasising that the packages currently available through on-line vendors vary considerably in their quality. We have already touched on some of the problems. Most important, today's on-line retrieval software is still unwieldy and difficult to use. The expression 'user friendly' has become a modern cliché, often deployed as a kind of spoof on new technology jargon. But it is a phrase publishers need to keep constantly in mind. The fact remains that these new media have to be easy and comfortable to use if they are to make any kind of breakthrough with users. Friendliness is an important key and so far the on-line industry has suffered badly because of software that is tough and intimidating to use. Currently the end user of a database is often not the 'end reader'. In other words, the search software is so impenetrable that experienced information scientists or librarians are the people who conduct the searches and provide the required information to the people who need it, the so-called 'end readers'.

Off-line characteristics

How does CD-ROM compare with the facilities of on-line systems? It is obviously pointless to pretend that off-line databases are a completely different animal to their on-line counterparts. Some of the key elements are more or less identical, at least in general terms. For example, both systems offer very large stores of information, dwarfing conventional print-based provisions. Also, both use sophisticated software to enable the megabytes to be rapidly sifted for the answers a user is after. Both can be updated, although it is admittedly far easier to do this with on-line databases than off-line ones.

So there are clear similarities suggesting, perhaps, that on-line and off-line might be competing for the same market. Maybe, after all, CD-ROM is just another format for the familiar on-line product. If so, surely the same commercial disappointments that on-line vendors have already suffered awaits the pioneers of CD-ROM. However, a little closer examination tells a different story.

Broad similarities are sometimes misleading. Too often they suggest a likeness that does not really exist. For example, we might say that on-line and CD-ROM databases can both be 'huge'. This suggests a degree of similarity which actually cloaks a fundamental difference. Obviously if we think as book publishers do, we probably conclude that both on-line and off-line databases offer information products of effectively 'unlimited' sizes, even though one deals in gigabytes and the other in megabytes. After all, if we were snails living in a world where an inch was a long way, we might say that it is as far from London to Paris as it is from London to the moon. And, from a snail's point of view, that would be a fair way of looking at things. The important point here is that while both types of database offer vast storage compared to the printed page, the CD-ROM product has a strict limitation on size while the on-line database (for all practical purposes) does not. The contrast between limitation and no limitation is no superficial distinction. It is a fundamental difference.

We have already seen how a CD-ROM works. The total digital capacity of a disc is around 600 megabytes. This figure accounts for all the raw data that can be stored. In practical terms a substantial amount of room must be reserved for the index files which make rapid and sophisticated searches possible. This can cut the available database down to under 350 megabytes, depending on how extensive you decide to make the index. So, while we are still dealing with a prodigious amount of data storage, an immediate discipline is imposed. There is an upper limit to the product size. This is a way of saying that CD-ROMs are discrete information products, standing alone and independent of one another. Of course, a really big product could span two or more discs but it is inconvenient for users to have to switch between discs and impossible to maintain real coherence and integration in the product.

The really important idea, though, is that CD-ROMs are independent of one another. This is a stark contrast to the concept of on-line networking. We have already seen how 'gateway' technology is enabling on-line users to communicate with large numbers of different databases, often housed on widely separated host computers. Telebase's Easynet system, for example, makes over 800 databases available through just one portal. Growth in gateways suggests that public on-line databases might one day be a single mega-network, linked by gates through which users can move easily, exploring and correlating data in thousands of independent databases. Before even starting to address the massive technical problems involved, we should ask whether anyone would really want to be a part of such a worldwide accumulation of information. However, whether or not such total interconnection ever occurred, the idea that it is feasible emphasises the essentially organic structure of the on-line industry.

CD-ROM products are fundamentally different. They stand alone and would not seem naturally to form networks of data. This does not mean they cannot be networked. In fact, an American corporation called Online Computer Systems has just announced a local area network called Opti-Net, designed especially for CD-ROMs and WORMs. But networking CD-ROMs raises at least two serious problems.

First, the seek times for a stand-alone CD-ROM are slow compared to magnetic media. This is because the laser stylus has to move physically from one sector of the disc to another. Even if servo technology improves, the problem will always remain. In addition the transfer of data from an optical disc to a microcomputer is slower than from a magnetic disc. In practice this is not a matter for much concern. In general we are only talking of fractions of a second. However, although these problems are insignificant for stand-alone use, once the disc system is networked they may become serious. Just as in a system using magnetic storage media, multiple access will result in a slowing down in the response time and already fairly slow seek and transfer times may become totally unacceptable.

Second, CD-ROM drives with their easily changed disc and modest price tags, are designed as cheap, stand-alone technology. Users will want to flip from one disc to another much as they would open and close different reference books. There is, after all, no complicated and time-consuming logging on and off procedures like those hampering the easy use of on-line databases so switching databases is an encouragingly simple process. But this very mobility becomes a potential headache in a network. Inevitably when one user goes to the network expecting a particular database to be loaded, they will find that a colleague has just replaced it by another. The only solution would be to network a bank of CD-ROM drives each with a specific database permanently loaded. Of course there will be situations where a single database will be needed by a lot of people all the time. Here even the difficulties of access time may be worth a networked solution. But on the whole CD-ROM is an independent medium without the potential organic coherence of the on-line industry. For most conventional publishers, however, this is a familiar, even attractive limitation. Described in terms of their discrete, stand-alone qualities, CD-ROMs sound a lot like books.

This independent quality that CD-ROMs possess also frees us from one of the tyrannies of on-line databases: payment by connect time. Lengthy searches are extremely expensive. It is simply out of the question to indulge in any undirected exploration of the database. Of course, much of the time, we need specific answers to specific questions or the relevant information that determines the answer. In such cases on-line access works well. So long as you can battle through the log-on/log-off procedures and use the search software smoothly, the connect time charges can be kept down. But there is inevitably a pressure on users who know the longer they take with their enquiries the more it costs. What a contrast between this and a book! When you buy a book you can open it and keep it open for as long as you like without anyone asking you for more money. Looked at this way, a book is an excellent 'low-tech' analogue for an off-line database.

One of the delights of using a book is to browse through its pages, dipping into sections that arouse interest. Sometimes, through browsing or random 'flicking', we can stumble upon valuable information purely by chance or make important correlations between ideas and facts which we might never otherwise have made. This facility of being able to browse turns an information based product into a knowledge-based product. Imagine trying to do it with an on-line database! The connect time charges would be crippling and who, anyway, could browse in a relaxed fashion while knowing that the bill was growing ever larger. It would be like trying to read a newspaper in a taxi and finding your eyes constantly straying to the meter.

CD-ROM can also free users from the protracted agonies of logging on to an on-line database. It remains a great mystery why an information delivery medium founded on high technology is so difficult to contact by telephone. It might be amusing were it not for the tremendous frustration it causes. The result of the logging on problems is to deter people from going repeatedly in and out of the database. But CD-ROM has a simple answer to logging on. Just leave the device permanently switched on and users can come and go as they please, dipping into the database whenever they need to. Free of connect time worries, the CD-ROM does more than offer the fullest possible use of a database: it positively encourages it.

Another area in which on-line and CD-ROM databases seem to have common ground is search and retrieval software. Obviously, any kind of electronic database product needs it and we have already emphasised how crucial the software is in determining the overall quality of the product. This is true for on- and off-line databases alike. However, we have seen how acutely the on-line industry has suffered from the generally unfriendly software it offers and we have already touched on one of the main reasons. An on-line vendor may be selling over 100 databases all mounted on a single host computer. The big US vendor, Dialog, has over 250. To handle access to each of these, the vendor, for economic reasons, has had to offer a single, general-purpose software package. It has always been impractical to tailor the software to suit particular databases aimed at particular markets. So the generalised software, having to cope with a range of features and requirements, has become difficult and complex to use. In CD-ROM publishing, this problem need not arise. If on-line publishing is really about niche information markets, then CD-ROMs are about niches in niches. In other words they can be highly specific, targetted at very precise market segments. There is no reason why the software accompanying the CD-ROM cannot be tailored very closely to the requirements of the particular database. It may of course mean that the software is adapted from original, general-purpose on-line software but the adaption could transform its friendliness.

So CD-ROMs need not suffer from the defects of on-line software. Worryingly, however, the evidence so far is that too little attention is being paid to this key area. Microcomputer versions of established mainframe packages are appearing and the first CD-ROM publishers are using them without paying enough attention to the damage they may do to the whole future of the off-line industry. The potential for a giant leap forward in database accessibility is there if publishers are ready to grasp the importance of making their product friendly. The aim should be to make the user forget the technology altogether and become absorbed in the experience of exploring the database with freedom and ease.

Finally, we can see a clear area of contrast between on- and off-line products. When we considered the key elements in on-line provision, we emphasised the importance of timeliness in the value of the information to the database users. As we saw, on-line databases can be kept literally up to the minute. Such highly current information sounds like a really persuasive sales feature but in reality, of course, it only answers an extremely specialised need. Most people will say they need up-to-date information and everyone means something different when they say it. For example, a currency dealer survives in business by knowing how exchange rates are fluctuating almost second by second. The information he uses has to be so up to date that data can turn from being valuable to worthless in seconds. Yesterday's exchange rates might as well come from the last century. This is an extreme. But much financial data is highly volatile and its value decays rapidly with time so the updating capabilities of an on-line system is vital. In fact, it can make some kinds of on-line databases virtually indispensable.

Although this kind of frantic requirement has a special excitement, most of us can make do with much less frequent updates than we think. Ask an information user whether he wants annual updates and he may say 'okay'. Ask if six-monthly would be better and he will nod vigorously. Offer monthly updates and he will beam with pleasure. Weekly updates will leave him speechless with delight. Then ask him to pay progressively more for the increasing frequency of updating and you will find out what he really needs. The chances are that a six-monthly or quarterly updating cycle will serve perfectly well. The reality is that very few people need information more recent than this.

This suggests a natural division between on-line and off-line applications. A CD-ROM is certainly updatable but at best on a monthly cycle. The mechanics are not difficult but it does need a remastering and re-replication of the disc. The less frequently this is done the better. An on-line database can be as readily updated on a daily basis as a monthly one. It is a medium that lends itself to fast changes. So we can easily imagine on-line dealing with information that is valuable only if it is constantly refreshed and CD-ROM with more stable data whose value falls off only gradually with time.

There is perhaps a brief postscript to add. We have said little about graphics. Increasingly, the issue of graphics-handling capabilities is becoming important. Up to now the database industry has been noticeably quiet about graphics largely because they would have to own up to having made little or no progress on the issue for nearly twenty years. The on-line database of today, just like the on-line database of yesterday, consists of almost exclusively textual information. CD-ROM has helped to focus the interest of innovators on the first real chance to create text-with-graphics databases. We have already seen how illustrated CD-ROMs are already being created, some even embodying an audio element. Of course, CD-I, which we consider in more detail in a later chapter, brings the notion of an integrated audio-visual database to life completely. But real problems remain. For CD-ROM in particular, the difficulty is not one of encoding graphics and text together but the problem of requiring non-standard display architecture to access the material. There are also questions of how to index graphic information so that the search and retrieval software can work effectively. But despite these problems, the embryonic off-line industry at least seems to be shaping up to the whole issue. The same cannot be said of on-line publishers. Perhaps this is just a way of emphasising that typical on-line products should be text only.

On-line and off-line products

We can now try to summarise the features that best characterise on-line and off-line products. Clearly there is overlap and plenty of room for interpretation. However, the features of the two kinds of database do give broad indications about the products that make the most sense for each.

What can we say about a model on-line database? It will be very large, typically of the order of gigabytes. It will consist entirely of text. The information on the database will be volatile, needing very frequent updating to maintain its inherent value to users. The content of the information will be specific. It will address tightly focused professional or academic needs. Finally, in terms of its comprehensiveness, timeliness and search facilities, the database product will offer very high value to its users.

The specification of a typical CD-ROM product would sound very similar. However, the database would be smaller, typically no larger than 400 megabytes. This may mean it would be less cosmically comprehensive than an on-line product. While it will probably consist mainly of text, it may include some graphics options too. The content will be relatively stable, requiring no more than quarterly updates. The type of information may encourage browsing rather than tightly directed search strategies. Like an on-line database, the CD-ROM has to offer high value but increasingly as the installed base of drives grows and standardisation makes compatability commonplace, information users may well build a library of CD-ROMs much in the way they would once have developed a collection of reference books. In other words, information users will in future see each CD-ROM as a particular reference tool among many such tools, rather than as one magic tool to solve all their information problems. Individually, each CD-ROM will be perceived as requiring less commitment than taking out an on-line subscription and so be purchased in a more relaxed, even casual fashion.

Quite clearly, these two pictures of on-line and CD-ROM products are highly simplified. But whether you agree with them in detail or not, they emphasise that the two types of database can coexist without one threatening the future of the other. In practice they represent two allied but different kinds of information product. Indeed, perhaps the first real off-line alternatives to massive on-line products will inject a new energy into the whole information industry and get established practitioners to re-examine the ways they approach their markets and their products.

5

How do you make a CD-ROM?

Making a CD-ROM is much easier than deciding to make it. Compared with sifting the conceptual and commercial problems facing would-be CD-ROM publishers, the production issues are refreshingly direct. But, at the same time, they are not issues to take lightly. Today's conventional print-based publishers, having already come to terms with recent revolutionary changes in book production techniques, may think they know a thing or two about computer technology. Optical disc publishing, however, has special and subtle complexities that wait for the unwary like a pike for the minnow.

Just as in any production process, the implications of errors are serious. But, in CD-ROM production, the dangers go beyond the mechanical. They can quickly threaten the editorial foundations of the product. Although a CD-ROM is very different from a computer software product, it has one strong similarity. Compare a computer program to a book like the one you are reading now. A few typographic errors here and there will not seriously affect the power of the book to do its job communicating whatever it has to say. But even a single error in a computer program can ruin it. The program may simply fail to run. Instead of a flawed product like a book with spelling mistakes, you have no product at all.

Clearly, CD-ROMs are not really like computer programs and this analogy is not an exact one. However, it emphasises that there are many more fatal traps to fall into in making a CD-ROM than in making a book. The potential for disaster is considerable. But unlike a computer program, the failure is unlikely to mean that the product just fails to function at all. It may be useable. It may work in a mechanical sense. Where it may fail totally is in delivering to the customers the kind of powerful information tool they are expecting.

The project team

Usually book editors are in tight control of the way their product develops without knowing or caring exactly how it is being typeset, printed and bound. However, where CD-ROM is concerned, proper editorial control demands real involvement in technical production issues. Indeed, distinctions between editorial, design and production functions blur. Publishers considering CD-ROM projects have to recognise they cannot rely on existing in-house skills and demarcations alone. The traditional ways will not work. A new kind of project team is needed with a fresh approach to project management. It is impossible to set out firm rules or recommendations for such a team. But we can say what it must be able to do. It has to be able to sift and evaluate highly technical issues to do with data structures and information management without losing sight of how the CD-ROM will ultimately be used. Through all the complexities, the team must remember their customer and their customer's needs. This also means trying to see the final product through the customer's eyes. How will the database 'feel' in use? What will it look like?

A very clear requirement is for the team to combine the technical, editorial, design and commercial flair needed for the success of a CD-ROM project. One of the key problems in a conventional publishing house is getting editors, designers and production controllers to think beyond conventional book and journal work. This broader perspective is essential if we are going to avoid a generation of CD-ROMs which are no more than direct transcriptions of print products to a digitised format. So the team must have flair and skill but it must also be able to work imaginatively outside the confines of the printed page.

CD-ROM production

An easy way out of the problems of making a CD-ROM is to get someone else to do it for you. There are already a number of companies in Europe and America supplying a full facility service. You tell them what product you want and provide them with a database in print or digitised form and they will prepare and load the database, provide software and have your disc mastered and replicated. Of course, this does not provide all the solutions. It is often difficult to predict the price of working with these kinds of suppliers, and publishers taking this route will have to accept a degree of uncertainty about how much the exercise will ultimately cost them. In addition it is vital that there are good communications between publisher and supplier about what the product needs to be and what it is turning out to be. This is an area fraught with dangers and simple misunderstandings can lead to serious even terminal difficulties.

We will return to the concept of the one-stop service later but it is worth observing that although buying someone else's time and skill can be a quick and simple way of producing your first CD-ROM products, it does little to improve your own knowledge of the medium. Publishers have to take their own view but clearly, if they foresee a long term future in optical disc markets, they will need at some stage to gain know-how about all the processes involved in developing and manufacturing the products. This is an obstacle which will have to be surmounted at some stage; avoiding it now only stores it up for later.

Whoever actually does the work, we can identify five key steps in CD-ROM production: choosing the database; capturing the data; producing the database; preparing the database and pre-mastering; mastering and manufacture. We will examine each of these briefly in turn.

Choosing the database

At the outset publishers have to take a basic decision. Are they going to use an existing printed database as the starting point or are they going to start from scratch and create an original product conceived from the first as a CD-ROM? Clearly the idea of creating a new publication that takes full account of all the particular strengths of the CD-ROM medium sounds most attractive. However, CD-ROM databases are very large so the task of drawing together the information for an original product would be formidable. In the present immature state of the CD-ROM market, it is hard to imagine any publisher undertaking the massive amount of work involved purely to create a CD-ROM. An original product would also have to be justified in other formats such as on-line and print-based. Otherwise the publisher would have no hope of recovering his development costs.

So the most likely route for publishers is to utilise printed databases to which they have electronic publishing rights or databases which are already in an on-line form. It is no surprise to see on-line vendors among the first to experiment with CD-ROM products. Although selling off-line versions of on-line products may seem a confusing strategy in marketing terms, there are substantial cost advantages. Having a database already on-line, effectively leapfrogs a number of important and expensive initial stages in CD-ROM production. Most conventional publishers are not also on-line vendors. There are of course exceptions. Perhaps the best known is Grolier. Starting with the print-based version of their *Academic American Encyclopaedia*, they first made it available on-line through a number of hosts and then produced a CD-ROM version which has become the CD-ROM equivalent of a bestseller. For most publishers, however, the starting point is a study of the print products they already publish.

It may look as if every major reference book publisher is sitting on a CD-ROM gold-mine. Certainly many of the facilities companies, eager to talk publishers into investing in CD-ROM, seem to think so. Indeed conventional publishers, new to the issues of electronic publishing, may share the view. Surely the large number of important printed works of reference are the perfect starting point for a whole range of CD-ROM products? Perhaps, but the key question is whether the publisher owns or controls the rights to exploit his properties in this way. Many major reference publications were conceived at a time when the electronic delivery of information was in its infancy. So authors and contributors may have granted the publisher a licence only controlling printed volume rights or at best a licence package including many possible exploitations but leaving out electronic delivery. If this is the case, it may still be possible for the publisher to negotiate the rights he needs for a CD-ROM product. However, the important point is that a publisher cannot assume he is free to make a CD-ROM out of a database simply because he publishes it in book or journal form.

Leaving aside how you source the database, there are some important considerations determining the choice of the right kind of database for the CD-ROM medium. First, CD-ROMs offer a massive volume of storage compared to printed materials. The maximum database size is nearly 400 megabytes, depending on the room needed for such things as index files. So while databases of a few megabytes in size can of course be distributed as CD-ROM, it makes little economic sense to do so. The cost of creating the CD-ROM is unlikely to be recovered from such a comparatively small product and the advantages of CD-ROM over microfilm or print are not so striking. In practice, the typical CD-ROM database will be between 100 and 350 megabytes and you need to select the subject of a CD-ROM publication accordingly.

The second consideration you must keep in mind concerns the currency of the information you are selling. We have already seen that CD-ROM is far less easily updated than on-line databases. Any updated version of a disc will need time for the data preparation, pre-mastering, mastering, replication and, lastly, the sending of new discs to subscribers. Realistically, a turnaround time of at least one month is needed for this kind of process. Obviously, depending on the requirements of the particular database, the time needed could be much longer. The main point is that CD-ROMs cannot compete with on-line provision of up-to-the-minute information. Volatile financial data, for example, are totally unsuited to CD-ROM. So you need to choose the kind of database which is relatively stable, requiring additions or revisions, say, quarterly or six-monthly.

Third, the database must be one that gains in value by being searchable in different ways. If the material only ever needs to be accessed by referring to one or two fixed criteria, such as a book catalogue always accessed via author and title, it would probably be better suited to microfilm storage. CD-ROM (and on-line) come into their own when there are ten or twenty search criteria or when users want to search the full text of the database.

Fourth, it is worth bearing in mind how frequently the information is likely to be used. It does not matter whether one person dips into it often or a lot of different people each use it only occasionally. If it is the kind of data that someone will be accessing often, CD-ROM will be an attractive medium. Because it is an off-line system no costly connect charges are being incurred and the database can be left switched on all day. Users can come and go as they please. There are no lengthy logging on and logging off procedures and you do not have to rely on the vagaries of the telephone system for getting in touch with the product.

There are of course other issues affecting the choice of the best kind of database for distribution by CD-ROM and the foregoing examples just touch on some of the most important factors. The key idea is to select the database most directly suited to the strengths of the medium.

Capturing the data

The substance of the eventual database could typically be available in three forms. First, it could already exist in machine-readable form, perhaps as magnetic tape for inputting to typesetting systems. The ideal situation would be if the database were already being distributed on-line. However, this is unlikely to be the case for most publishers and we will ignore the possibility in what follows. Second, it may exist only in printed or typewritten form. Third, it may comprise in whole or in part, illustrations which, obviously, cannot be keyboarded.

If a database already exists in machine-readable form, the capture of the data is more or less achieved without further work. In practice, if the data is in the form of typesetting tapes, some problems may arise later because of embedded typesetting codes. These codes control the typesetting process but can cause real confusion in the searching of a CD-ROM database. Usually they will need to be stripped out leaving a more or less neutral database.

If the database is purely textual but is not in machine-readable form, there are basically two possibilities. Either someone has to laboriously keyboard all the material and store it on magnetic discs or tape, or it can be scanned by an OCR system. OCR stands for 'Optical Character Recognition'. It allows textual information to be scanned and digitised character by character. Both keyboarding and OCR are extremely expensive procedures, especially for databases of the size normally chosen for CD-ROM distribution. The only other alternative is to use the system that would be needed if the database included illustrations.

The only practical way of digitising illustrations is to use a scanning system that effectively captures entire facsimile images of pages. If OCR capture of textual information is really too costly to be contemplated then this full-page scanning can also be used for text data. The way the process works is to convert the graphics or type on a page into a series of small elements called pixels. Each of these is given a digital code which identifies it as either black or white. The digital coding therefore represents an overall black and white facsimile of the scanned page. Although much cheaper than OCR for text, this type of scanning has major drawbacks in CD-ROM development.

First and most obvious is the problem of search and retrieval. If the database is made up of facsimile images of pages, the text on each of those pages cannot be searched. Each page would need to be manually indexed. Retrieval would then follow searches based only on keywords. Second, this type of scanning is very expensive on memory. Even though a CD-ROM has a huge capacity, storing full-page facsimiles dramatically reduces the database that can be accommodated. The memory requirement is about forty times as great as for pages coded character by character. Approximately a quarter of a million A4 pages of textual data can be held on a CD-ROM normally. On a facsimile basis this is cut to around 6000 pages. The third disadvantage concerns the degree of resolution needed to interpret the facsimile pages. If high-resolution illustrations are included, the database will only be useable on hardware which includes the appropriate display architecture. This means the right kind of graphics card in the computer and a monitor of sufficient resolution to make sense of the images.

Producing the database

After capturing the data, the creative work can begin in earnest. Some of the work of producing the database from the machine-readable information may already have been done. After all, if the material comes from typesetting tapes or even edited typescript, it will embody a logical structure. It may be tempting to assume that this is an adequate way of organising the information. In reality it is likely to be a reasonable way of organising a printed work of reference rather than a major electronic database.

The objective in creating the database is to plan and organise the records and files to make them rapidly accessible by suitable search and retrieval software. In most cases the aim will be to offer free text retrieval. There is a range of proprietary retrieval packages already available. Most are derivatives of on-line systems, modified for use with microcomputers. Some can be tailored specifically to suit the purposes of a particular CD-ROM product. But the important point for publishers is that preparing the database must be carried out in close consultation with the retrieval software vendors.

The planning work with the software experts will include a full analysis of the content of the database and how potential customers may wish to use it. The structure of the database can then be decided so that, for example, related data is grouped close together. It is often possible to anticipate the user's likely search patterns and arrange the data to minimise search times; always an impressive sales feature in this kind of product. Careful planning can totally disguise the limitation on search times imposed by the disc's CLV mode of replay. It is also essential to consider the kind of people who are most likely to use the database. Knowing the customer is vital if you are to design the best means for the customer to use the product. What will appear on the screen and how will it look? If users are unfamiliar with computer technology, can we keep the search software friendly and easy to use? To make the best of powerful search technique, a command structure is best. But commands mean users have to learn vocabulary and syntax. If they are intimidated by the command structure they may never get into the database to see what an excellent resource it is. An alternative is to use a menu-driven approach. This is simpler but less powerful. Perhaps a compromise can be created, a hybrid of commands and menu options. These are the kinds of issues that vitally affect the quality of the end product. It is crucial that publishers devote real effort to coming up with the right solutions if CD-ROMs are to have any hope of long-term success.

Once these planning issues have been thoroughly explored and completely resolved, the database has to be divided up into logical elements. The substance of the elements varies of course from database to database. In an encyclopaedia they are likely to be articles made up of extensive text files. Each will need to be subdivided into smaller building blocks designed to meet the needs of the application. This is fairly familiar editorial ground to anyone who has worked in reference publishing and the only additional consideration is the different ways the material may be searched by users and what this implies for the way the database is divided. In practice this means anticipating the needs of users and determining how, therefore, you are going to arrange the searchability of the database. For example, you have to decide whether all or just part of one of the main logical elements will be searchable. If you decide only parts can be searched, you can still allow the rest to be retrievable. Finally, you have to define what is called a 'stop list'. This is a collection of common words such as 'with', 'but', 'and', which can be ignored during a search to prevent the process being slowed down unnecessarily.

Before the database can be loaded onto a magnetic medium, the software vendor will need to arrange a formatting process and, lastly, the formatted data has to be inverted. The term 'inverted' has here a technical meaning. In the context of a database it has little to do with turning anything inside out or upside down. The inversion involves processing every record in the database. In each one, every significant word in every searchable element is stored with an appropriate locator. This process builds up a massive additional piece of data known as an 'occurrence list' or 'inverted file'. All that now needs to be done is to create the master magnetic tape from which the CD-ROM master is produced.

Preparing the database

The magnetic tape from which the CD-ROM is mastered is a kind of reflection of the CD-ROM itself. Fundamental to the process is the creation of a directory containing information about every file in the database. If the database was going to be delivered on-line, the structure of the directory would be determined by the operating system of the chosen host computer. On a CD-ROM we have to rely on the formulation of an international standard telling us how the directory and the files should be structured. We have seen that encouraging progress is being made towards an accepted standard and most disc producers today would be following the proposals of the High Sierra Group in the reasonable belief they will soon be accepted more or less in their entirety.

The appropriate directory and file structure can be created using a special computer program designed for the purpose. Several proprietary packages are available. Once complete, the database has to be reconstituted into sectors and blocks that match the way data is laid down on a CD-ROM complete with headers, synchronisation and error detection and correction codes. Finally, the resulting database is recorded onto high quality magnetic tape and delivered to a convenient mastering facility.

Mastering and manufacture

The mastering and replication process has to be carried out in 'clean room' conditions. This means making certain no dust, excessive humidity or sudden changes of temperature can corrupt the process. The facilities needed are complex and costly and no CD-ROM publisher is ever likely to want or to need to invest the huge sums involved to create their own mastering plant. However, the process of manufacturing CD-ROMs is basically very similar to making audio disc products so the meteoric rise of the compact disc music market has had important implications for CD-ROM producers. In fact, there have been both benefits and problems.

The immediate benefit of course has been to get mastering and replication technology onto a mass-market footing. This has meant increasing numbers of mastering locations throughout the world and greater geographical choice for CD-ROM producers. It has also meant some worthwhile cost benefits from the economies of scale created by the high volume demands of the audio industry. But those very demands have also created difficulties for CD-ROM publishers. The music business has boomed so dramatically that until recently all the available mastering plants were working flat out just to keep up with demand. Understandably the people running these expensive facilities were only really interested in stamping out the millions of audio discs for this huge and lucrative market. Asking them to produce a run of a hundred or so copies of a CD-ROM was like asking a printer engaged in mass-market paperback production to slip in a work on Egyptian hieroglyphics. Today the pressure on the mastering plants from the audio market is still high but the number of plants has grown and the delays that a CD-ROM publisher might once have experienced are now no longer a serious problem.

The technicalities of the mastering process need not concern us. Suffice to say that it is highly technical and recent years have seen great strides made in quality control so that CD-ROM producers can be confident that if their master magnetic tape is right, their CD-ROM will work without problems. Obviously, however, it is vital to ensure that the tape sent to the mastering facility is in fact right in every detail. Usually, before going all the expensive way with the mastering process, a check disc is produced rather like a final proof of a book. It has a limited lifetime and cannot be used as a master to replicate copies. But it allows the publisher and software team to test the disc thoroughly to make sure their product works in the way they had planned. Once the 'proof' is approved, the final master is created. A negative shell of nickel is made from the master: this is usually called the 'father'. From this a number of positives or 'mothers' are produced and from each of these a number of (negative) 'sons' are made. The sons are in fact the stampers from which the production run of discs is created. The plastic surface of the replicated discs is finally given a reflective coating and a protective outer coating. The last process includes punching out the centre hole, labelling the disc and packaging it.

Costs

The costs of CD-ROM manufacture have always been a vexed question. Many of the facilities companies claiming to offer a one-stop service to would-be publishers would in the past get a bit vague when costs were mentioned. Today the position is much clearer. Philips, for example, will give detailed example costs for the mastering process, including data preparation if you want them to do that for you. The real difficulties come in estimating pre-production costs. Data capture, for example, could be a massively expensive process if a 300 megabyte database has to be keyboarded from scratch. The time taken in database design and the elaborate consultations with software companies can also become a major element. The actual cost of the licence to use a proprietary software package is a matter of negotiation but at this early stage of the game many software vendors are keen to see their systems established in the market place and are often ready to do helpful royalty-based deals. Obviously a simple answer is for a publisher to go to a one-stop facilities company who will quote a price for a package job. You still have to be careful to ensure you know exactly what you are getting for your money and you will inevitably remain an outsider in the development process, learning comparatively little about the detailed skills needed to create a good CD-ROM product. Individual publishers will have their own view about this. One-stop shopping certainly has some beguiling attractions.

What is clear about CD-ROM costing is that there are very large fixed costs associated with this kind of product and this cost must somehow be amortised by the volume of sales. Realistically

CD-ROM markets are still niches in niches. Few discs are likely to sell more than one or two hundred copies. The Grolier disc, however, with sales of over two thousand is stunning proof that there are always exceptions to this gloomy kind of forecasting. Clearly, leaving aside the possibility of an occasional breakthrough, the market is low volume and that means high end-user pricing.

Philips recently provided some manufacturing costs which can serve as some guide at least to the final stages of CD-ROM production. The costs were intended by Philips as a guide and anyone seriously interested in costing out a CD-ROM product must check with Philips or other suppliers to get up-to-date figures. The figures given here certainly do not represent the exact costs from Philips at the time this book reaches your hands.

CD-ROM MANUFACTURE

Number of discs:	**10**	**50**	**250**	**500**	**1000**
Master disc:	£2200	£2200	£2200	£2200	£2200
Replication:	£270	£1100	£4000	£8000	£14,000
Total cost:	£2470	£3300	£6200	£10,200	£16,200
Unit cost:	£247	£66	£24.80	£20.40	£16.20

Philips also provided a rough estimate for preparing the data ready for mastering. For about 250 megabytes of data they quoted £9250.

Purely for curiosity, we can do a hypothetical sum to get some feeling for the kind of unit cost we may be looking at in a 'typical' CD-ROM product. Assume the cost of data capture and database design and creation comes to £35,000. For a 250 megabyte product this could be a modest estimate, especially if the data is not initially in machine-readable form. We can add to this the Philips' estimate for data preparation, adjusted for both inflation and Philips' optimism to £10,000. This brings the costs to £45,000. Assume we 'print' 250 copies. This costs a total of £6200. The overall total cost then is £51,200 which means a unit cost per disc of £204.80.

The above sum neatly sidesteps the question of what is included as a part of the capture and design and creation cost. Much of it may be attributed as overhead rather than direct cost. Nonetheless, however the numbers are regarded, there is a basic cost that has to be recovered by sales before a CD-ROM can have any hope of showing a margin. And if we are looking for a net contribution, we have to take account of substantial marketing and distribution costs which also have to be recovered from sales.

Of course we have performed a piece of purely hypothetical arithmetic which may do no more than prove we can count. However, as a rough guideline it gives an idea of the type of commercial problem we face in CD-ROM publishing. After all, if we start with a unit cost of £200 on a product, we will undoubtedly be pricing it to end users at several times this figure. Together with the hardware complications, this points to one very basic requirement. The information product itself has to represent very high value to potential customers if it is to stand any chance of commercial success.

6

Markets for CD-ROM

We have already touched on the difficulties the on-line industry has experienced trying to sell big database products. The sufferings of on-line vendors over the years has culminated in huge stores of largely unused information clogging gigabytes of computer storage. It has been a story of products in pursuit of markets. The starting point was clever technological innovation. Computer and telecommunication technology seemed poised to offer brilliant new opportunities to all kinds of information consumers. Crucially the consumers were never really consulted. The opportunities for consumers were seen by the people needing to sell their product and that is the wrong way round. It is like an estate agent trying to sell a house to someone who does not need it or want it. He is saying, 'please spend a large sum of money because I know what you want and what you like and what will make you happy.' The estate agent of course would have no more luck than the on-line industry.

But surely the off-line industry is different? CD-ROM is, after all, a distinct and new medium. Perhaps. But the similarities between CD-ROM products and on-line products are striking. They are generically close. In addition the technology is glamorous and exciting. Potential CD-ROM producers are enthusiasts. All the danger signs are there. Are we about to see another deluge of good-looking products all searching for non-existent markets?

There is a good deal of talk these days about niche markets. No-one has ever really defined what niche markets are but the implication is that they are very small. They are presumably little slices cut out of broad generic markets. They are highly specialised. Of course there is nothing new about the idea of niches. Many publishers make good money from publishing books for these small but easily identifiable groups of customers. However, while on-line products have been described as reaching niche markets, CD-ROM products have been said to be suited to niches within niches. This is surely a pessimistic view. How small does a niche become before you are creating one copy of your product for the one person in the world who has asked for it? We have to take the view that CD-ROM will in some real sense address generic markets. That means more than a handful of potential customers. If CD-ROMs cannot do this, it is hardly worth conventional publishers wasting their time finding out about them.

It is pointless to attempt any quantitative discussion of CD-ROM markets at present. The markets are too embryonic to make sense of this kind of analysis beyond saying that if your product is aimed at lawyers, knowing how many there are will help in estimating potential sales. It is best to stick to a qualitative approach. Nor is it possible to be comprehensive in examining market possibilities. New ideas are appearing all the time and that is as it should be in an innovative and entrepreneurial business. It would be plainly hopeless to try to cover everything that has already emerged and everything that may yet emerge. What we can do instead is to touch on some key areas where broad generic markets already exist for large-scale information products and explore some ideas as to how CD-ROM might find a place in these markets. We will start by looking at professional markets such as medicine and law. Then we will examine the possibilities of CD-ROM in education, followed by applications in business. Finally we will consider whether the home can ever represent a serious CD-ROM market.

CD-ROMs in medicine

The world of medical databases is dominated by the US National Library of Medicine's huge database of abstracts from medical literature. The database, called 'Medline', has been available on-line for some years and plays a vital role in a field where the literature expands at a frightening rate. 'Medline' has to try to cover more than 4500 journals with several gigabytes of new information appearing every month. It is a vital information tool and is an obvious, almost inevitable on-line database product. As a result, it is the second most successful database in the world in terms of the number of people searching it. (The most successful is the legal database, 'Lexis'.)

Perhaps it is not surprising that such a huge database is difficult to search. The software for the purpose is complex and intimidating and, on the whole, few medical professionals search 'Medline' themselves. They have to rely on specially trained staff who do little else apart from carrying out specified searches. A bold effort to make 'Medline' more readily accessible is being planned using CD-ROM. The proprietors of 'Medline', Mead Data Central, are working with Micromedex of Denver, Colorado who already have a CD-ROM product line and are now an operating division of Mead. Their plan is to put 'Medline' on CD-ROMs with the intention that it should be used by medical professionals rather than information experts. It is hard to know what to make of Mead's indifference to the potential clash with their on-line product. Clearly they take the view that there is something to be gained in having the same product delivered both on- and off-line. However, Mead appear to have been beaten to the post by Horizon Information Services of Los Angeles and Cambridge Scientific Abstracts of Bethesda, both of whom have recently announced CD-ROM versions of 'Medline'. Horizon's product contains 300,000 records and their subscription charges, ranging between $3500 and $4700, include disc drives and quarterly updates. Horizon plan to reduce the update cycle to an ambitious one month. The retrieval software has been designed to be simple; 'for the end user rather than the professional searcher' as Horizon's literature puts it. Cambridge offer a database of 239,000 records for $6350 including the drive. Updates are quarterly.

Micromedex are CD-ROM pioneers in the medical field. They were the first to issue medical databases and today offer a major package called the 'Computerised Clinical Information System' (CCIS). It originated as a mainframe database and is now offered as a group of independent but interrelated CD-ROMs. The components of the CCIS are four large databases, each housed on a single disc. *Drugdex* is what Micromedex term an 'up-to-date and unbiased, referenced drug information system'. Thousands of drugs are evaluated, indexed by US and foreign brand names, diseases and associated drug information terms. *Emergindex* is a clinical information system indexed via a 40,000 word medical thesaurus. *Identidex* is a unique tablet and capsule identification system with around 23,000 entries. Using it, physicians can make identifications using either manufacturers' imprinted codes or physical characteristics such as colour, size and shape. Finally, *Poisindex* is a huge toxicology database designed to help identify and provide key information on more than 300,000 substances. In 1986 the whole package was available for $7500 for a year's subscription including quarterly updates.

Another American company, Digital Diagnostics, specialising in medical CD-ROMs is working closely with physicians at the Johns Hopkins University and the famous Mayo Clinic to devise a database product for practising doctors. The new product will be called *BiblioMed* and it will cover the same kind of ground as 'Medline' without being so cosmic in its comprehensiveness. The company's medical advisers will select specific articles for inclusion based on their direct interest to medical practitioners. The finished product will feature search and retrieval software chosen especially because it is easy to use. The plan is to offer the disc at a price within reach of the individual physician, around $1800 for a year with quarterly updates. As usual in these kinds of deals, hardware is extra.

So far then, the products available follow predictable lines. It is too early to say whether these kinds of CD-ROMs are making a real impact. However, what many medical professionals may be waiting for is more innovative CD-ROM applications. A number of exciting projects are said to be under way. These include using CD-ROM as a teaching medium by combining textual data with audio (such as heart sounds) and illustrations and so creating powerful diagnostic tools. Other possibilities are using CD-ROM to store X-ray and brain scan data.

Using CD-ROMs in the law

If medicine has the second most successful on-line database in its ranks, the law can boast the most successful one of all. Mead Data Central are again the vendors and the database is 'Lexis'. The only competitor worldwide is West Publishing's 'Westlaw'. The British run legal database 'Eurolex' was closed down in 1986. In fact, outside the United States, lawyers have remained indifferent to the attractions of on-line access to European case law files which are nowadays included in 'Lexis'. The British law publishers, Butterworth, acting as Mead's agents, attracted a good deal of pungent criticism for buying the 'Eurolex' operation and then immediately closing it down. Since then, estimates suggest that Butterworth have found fewer than 150 British subscribers to the 'Lexis' service. It is not surprising that Mead, who opened their own international headquarters in London in 1984, retrenched to Ohio two years later. The fragmentation of the European law markets where legal systems run on broadly national lines, together with the traditional dependence of European lawyers on paper rather than high technology, suggests on-line systems will make little profitable impact in Europe for some time to come. Until then, British case law remains available on-line but only from Mead's 'international office' in Ohio.

Despite its performance outside the United States, there is little doubt that 'Lexis' is one of the few real success stories of the on-line industry. While no breakdowns are available, it seems clear that the 'Lexis' database contributes the lion's share to Mead's $200 million annual revenue. Yet up to now virtually no work has been done on using CD-ROM, either for derivatives of 'Lexis' or for other legal applications and what little has been done has been in the United States. Most surprising of all, the development work has not come from such giants as Mead, but from virtual unknowns in the database publishing business.

Time Management Software (TMS) based in the small town of Stillwater, Oklahoma, is best known as a top class facilities company active in both video disc and CD-ROM projects. They have their own search software which has been used on a number of products. To demonstrate the power of the software, TMS has made three CD-ROMs that could be of direct use to lawyers. They have created full-text databases out of three of the codes from the US Code of Federal Regulations. These are the Internal Revenue Code, the Public Health Code and the Social Security Code. So far, TMS have only used the discs as demonstration vehicles for their software but would make them commercially available should any demand become evident.

The only State Code in the United States on disc is the Code of the Commonwealth of Virginia, produced by the Michie Company, a small legal publishing company. All other State Codes, apart from that of Hawaii, are available as on-line databases and no-one seems to be hurrying to create more CD-ROM versions.

Some experimental projects are under way but most organisations seem to be waiting to see what Mead and West do with the anticipated CD-ROM products derived from their existing on-line databases. One major product under discussion by a loose consortium of companies is a 'professional office' package of several reference tools on a single disc. The idea is a little like Microsoft's *Bookshelf* which we have already described. In a legal context, the disc might offer the State Code, a database related to the area of law in which the office specialises, a legal dictionary plus a variety of applications and standard form generating software.

So far there is some talk but no action and the legal market worldwide, a seemingly obvious testing ground for CD-ROM, remains largely untried.

CD-ROMs and education

The education market and, in particular, the market in schools has for long mesmerised new media publishers. Of course, technology in education is not new. Overhead projectors, film loop machines, slide projectors and, more recently, video tape recorders have been playing some part in the teaching or learning process. Most of this audio visual equipment is now gathering dust and many teachers will still argue that there is no substitute for 'talk and chalk'.

Although our main focus is CD-ROM, we need to spend a few moments reflecting on educational computing. It provides a useful insight into the problems high technology media can meet in the classroom. The UK experience is especially interesting since all the early indicators suggested that computers would quickly become an integral part of educational provision. In the late 1970s, the British government established the Microelectronics Education Programme (MEP) to prepare the way for educational computing. It provided teacher training, technical support to schools, curriculum centres where prototype software could be developed and, supposedly, a stimulus for commercial publishers to get involved in educational software. At the same time, schools were given funds to help buy hardware and a machine especially designed by Acorn Computers — the now famous BBC Microcomputer — quickly dominated the market.

From a publishing point of view, the situation looked promising. A clear and coherent government initiative; money for hardware; a single machine base dominating — all suggested a good basis for investing in software development. Most of the major educational publishing houses quickly got to work. It seemed a natural and attractive addition to their traditional book publishing activities. Today, a few years later, virtually all the major houses have dropped out, some having suffered substantial losses. A few companies are still selling their backlist of titles but new product development from the big houses is minimal. In fact, most of the new software is coming from very small organisations, almost cottage industries, who, no doubt, can make some sense of the economics of the market in a way that larger companies cannot. Educational computing in the UK has not dramatically affected the way schools run or the classes they offer. If it came in with a bang, it is going out with a whimper.

What went wrong? The idea of computers doing something useful such as teaching people things caught the imagination of educationalists, parents, hardware manufacturers and publishers. There was even real optimism that educational software aimed at the home would at last displace the much derided computer game. The home market turned out to be as much of a pipe-dream as the school market. The sad difference was that publishers lost even more money producing software for homes than they did for schools.

The truth is that no-one knows exactly what went wrong in the school market. The disaster of the home market was easier to interpret and it has a message for optical disc publishers as well as software specialists. Whatever they may say in public, people do not want to educate themselves in the comfort of their own homes. They want to have fun. They want to be entertained. That is why television is such a successful mass opiate. The thing it does really well is provide undemanding, pleasurable ways of passing time.

Some of the factors that caused the false dawn in educational computing are clear. Even allowing for the special funding of hardware, the school market is a financially stricken one. Only when the patient was more or less dead did the British government make some special short-term funding available for software purchases. Up to then, they supported hardware but not the software that would make the hardware do anything useful. In addition, really good software cost a great deal of money to develop. With about 5000 secondary schools and just over 20,000 primary schools, the numerical market is small and this was coupled with the fact that it neither could nor was prepared to pay a commercial rate for the products. Selling the products to the schools was also a tough proposition. Software needs to be demonstrated. It cannot be given the 'flick test' like a book. A sales representative could spend hours demonstrating a product in order to get a sale of perhaps one or two packages. The revenue from the sale would not even pay for his shoe leather in making the call. The traditional inspection copy approach, so successful with textbooks where class set adoptions might follow, was a disaster in software. The cost of processing an inspection copy request was simply too high when all that might follow was a single copy order. In addition, after inspection copies were returned pirated copies began to appear.

One further problem which is difficult to quantify but is certainly a factor, is the fear harboured by teachers (along with people in other professions) of being displaced by technology. This is particularly true when children are plainly less intimidated by it than adults.

In the United States, a slow, fragmented and generally unpromising start has led to a much more successful situation. It is now quite clear that, despite the early misgivings of teachers, publishers are making money from educational software. One reason is pure arithmetic. There are many more schools and many more pupils than in the UK. The market is simply much bigger. Also, despite the problems of national spending priority which any education system suffers, it is a market with money. And a good deal of it can come from affluent parents, often sophisticated high-earners prepared to place pressure on their children's schools to make sure up-to-date measures like educational computing are implemented. Also they have, from the start, been using much more grown-up hardware than in Britain. Today Apple holds well over half the school market and virtually all the software available for schools is disc-based. A more persuasive reason for the health of American educational software is that the US system of education places greater emphasis on drill and practice and tutorial than the British system. In Britain, teachers demand open-ended software, simulations and database products. This kind of software is difficult and costly to develop. In the United States, the schools relish the kind of software that is easy and relatively cheap to produce. This is of course a sweeping generalisation and a gross injustice to the many excellent and innovative products that are the exceptions that prove the rule.

What can we learn from the troubled story of educational computing that will help CD-ROM producers? Quite obviously the biggest lesson is that education is an impoverished market. Asking schools to pay large sums for new hardware and software is a major problem no matter how exciting the product looks to them. Faced with the alternative of buying books or a CD-ROM system, they will inevitably (and quite rightly) choose books. The point is that the choice should never arise. It should never be a question of books or technology. The reality in underfunded education systems is, however, that such choices almost always have to be made unless special funds from other sources, such as parents, can be found. CD-ROMs also suffer from a disadvantage which computers never had. Everyone more or less agreed that the idea of computers in schools was 'a good thing'. After all the children would be growing up in a computerised society. They would need to be comfortable with computers. Perhaps it would be a good idea if they could program them too. Can you imagine anything similar being said about CD-ROM? What kind of future society could be CD-ROM-orientated? Why should children even need to know what a CD-ROM is? And, incidentally, just what *is* a CD-ROM anyway? In other words, there will be no general pressure from educationalists or parents to put CD-ROMs into schools. It may be a clever gadget but not an essential one.

Even if this problem did not exist, just what sensible applications can CD-ROM have in classrooms? Clearly, it could carry huge amounts of educational software but that would be relegating the medium to a kind of giant storage cabinet. The real opportunity would be to offer the children opportunities to browse through and explore massive databases in order to learn about the process of building up knowledge and extracting and correlating significant information. To some extent this can already be done using magnetic media. But if CD-ROM can also incorporate sound and illustrations (which it can), the database is not simply much bigger, it is far richer too.

Perhaps understandably, no real CD-ROM development has emerged for the education market as yet. However, a recent hardware innovation opens the door to some prospect of existing CD-ROMs finding their way into American classrooms at least. MicroTRENDS of Schaumburg, Illinois have recently developed a co-processor card for US education's most successful microcomputer, the Apple II. They call it the 'Jonathan card' and for $795 the card makes it possible to interface the Apple with a CD-ROM drive. For an additional $395, you can buy Jonathan CD which is the physical interface needed to accept the plug for the CD-ROM drive itself. Currently the only card available is designed for the Philips CM-100 drive though others may follow soon. MicroTRENDS have also announced a networking facility for Apples which will enable schools to run up to five student work stations from a single CD-ROM drive.

With admirable opportunism, the first to take advantage of Jonathan has been Grolier with their CD-ROM electronic encyclopaedia. MicroTRENDS have worked on a conversion of Grolier's existing access software to produce a version that suits the Apple environment. Grolier expect to find a substantial additional market in schools for their Apple-version disc and plan an aggressive marketing campaign. The electronic encyclopaedia, while not primarily aimed at the education market, is the first classroom CD-ROM product to be made available.

A few other nominally 'educational' discs do exist. For example, Cornell University's English Department has produced a disc database of fiction writing by black writers. Ibycus Systems use a CD-ROM as part of a system to help students and scholars working with classical languages such as Ancient Greek, Hebrew and Latin. Their disc contains the works of Homer, Sophocles, Plato, Aristotle and Plutarch. It also includes the Jewish Bible in Hebrew and Greek and a Greek version of the New Testament. Quite clearly, neither of these discs have any pretentions to being mainstream products.

An interesting and hopeful sign comes from at least one US School District. Montgomery County Public Schools were at the forefront of educational computing initiatives even before it became fashionable. Today the district is showing the same kind of energy with some CD-ROM experimentation. It has been running a test using a small number of disc drives in its schools and, if the results are encouraging, the district aims to have around 100 operating in their secondary schools by 1988.

At least one educational database on CD-ROM is commercially established but it is not aimed at classroom use. ORI of Bethesda, working with SilverPlatter, have just announced a disc version of the US National Institute of Education's ERIC database. More recently still, Dialog, the big US on-line vendor has also announced an ERIC disc. ERIC is in fact a combination of two databases: 'Resources in Education' (RIE) and 'Current Index to Journals in

Education' (CIJE). The product is a series of discs, each an archive of material spanning many years. The customers for this product will presumably be educationalists, administrators and researchers; the very people who currently use ERIC in its on-line form. Probably the reason ERIC is on disc has more to do with the fact that the data is in the public domain and therefore royalty free, than that the database is an obvious opportunity for the CD-ROM format.

Despite Grolier's excellent encyclopaedia, time may run out for CD-ROM in the classroom. Philips and Sony have already announced an evolution of CD-ROM which they call Compact Disc Interactive or CD-I. We have already mentioned CD-I briefly and we will consider it in more detail in the next chapter. However, it includes as its natural features, high quality illustrations, full-motion animations, audio and text. It will come in a player that needs no computer to control it and will play on an ordinary television rather than a costly monitor. It is principally intended as a consumer product but it may well have massive potential in education and training markets. Time will tell.

CD-ROMs in business

In the mid and late 1970s, business seminars and conferences were full of talk about office automation. Large corporations began to spend huge sums on integrated systems which they supposed would revolutionise their businesses. Networked work stations; word processing; database and spreadsheet software; laser printers — all the paraphernalia of office technology rapidly became a more pressing issue than more prosaic questions about the fundamentals of good business practice and whether a company was efficiently run (with or without wall-to-wall microcomputers). Perhaps we might all have learned some lessons from the technological revolutions of previous generations. Photocopiers for example had hardly transformed businesses except in terms of the vastly increased amount of waste paper generated by them. In retrospect it is astonishing how people supposed, naively, that new technology would work miracles without any other effort than buying the equipment and plugging it in. For example, it has taken years for businesses to come to grips with the question of how industrial relations and training are affected by automation.

What we now know by painful and expensive experience is that technology is only as good as the hands that hold it. No amount of microcomputing will turn a bad business decision into a good one. Any number of gigabytes of computer memory is worth trading for an innovative product idea or a truly creative and dynamic marketing plan. Ultimately the technology issues resolve themselves into issues about people and their basic business skills. Find an excellent manager and the technology will be put to good use and performance will benefit. Find a bad manager and he will remain bad with or without the technology.

All of this philosophising about office technology is really an expression of some optimism for CD-ROM in businesses. The most powerful tool in the hands of good business people is access to information. If technology can give increased or improved access to relevant information, then the technology will sell. And this is exactly what CD-ROM is geared to do. The budgets exist. The money is there waiting for the right products.

Moreover, CD-ROM as a niche market vehicle, will suit business environments very well. It does not take much imagination to think of dozens of specialised banks of information that would suit different types of business. In addition, it holds the promise of relatively low-cost access to massive stores of information. Up to now businesses have had to rely on a range of sources including news clipping agencies, market researchers and on-line services. Typically it has been the larger corporations that could afford to do the job well. But small companies are the norm. In the United States, for example, 57 per cent of all businesses employ less than ten people. If CD-ROM can truly show itself as a relevant, low-cost medium, it could make a major impact on this numerically large market place.

Surprisingly, there has been little sign to date of a big push into the business market by CD-ROM producers. The most important product, available in the United States, has actually been around for about two years which makes it a veteran in CD-ROM terms. Datatext have a four disc segmented database aimed purely at corporate markets. In fact the product is called, with admirable simplicity, the *Corporate Information Database*. The information is drawn from four main sources currently available on-line: the Business Research Corporation, Media General, Predicast and Disclosure databases. Over 10,000 companies are profiled from 900 lines of business in 50 different industries. For any company on the database, you can get all the data from the four primary sources at once. The disc's output can be directed to magnetic disc files in suitable formats for Wordstar, Multimate, or Lotus 1-2-3. Currently Datatext offer their product segmented into four broad business categories: consumer, industrial, technology and services. Each is available on a single disc at about $10,000 including a CD-ROM drive. Although very much a business tool, the databases are currently used by market analysts and market research agencies rather than individual medium and small-size businesses.

More recently Disclosure themselves have announced a CD-ROM product based on their well-established on-line products. We have already examined *Compact Disclosure* in an earlier chapter as an example of the growing diversity of CD-ROM products. But it is worth re-emphasising the trend among on-line vendors towards creating CD-ROM versions of their products. It is hard to tell whether this is for considered strategic reasons to do with confidence in CD-ROM's future or whether it is simply a bid to prop up the ailing on-line industry by a diversification which, after all, costs it relatively little to try.

If we are to believe Dr Roger Summit, President of the on-line giant, Dialog, it is certainly not a last throw of the dice. Dialog have just announced a commitment to produce a number of their databases on CD-ROM (Dialog OnDisc) and this could be interesting news for the business market. Summit was quoted recently in Learned Information's *Monitor* as saying, '. . . our overall mission has always been to provide increasingly effective means for accessing, presenting and disseminating recorded information through computer technology. With the market starting to accept CD-ROM technology, application of this technology to Dialog OnDisc is a natural evolution for us.'

It is too early to judge whether this kind of statement is an exercise in public relations or something more substantial. What is certain is that CD-ROM must go beyond these first generation derivative products if it is to have a long-term future. Putting on-line products onto disc may be an easy way forward, but has little point if it only attracts revenue that would otherwise be spent on-line. There has to be an impact on information consumers who have never used the services of outfits such as Dialog and Disclosure. Only in this way will the universe of electronic database users be genuinely enlarged. If this fails to happen, the ills of the on-line industry will simply be transferred to the new off-line one.

In pursuit of the home market

Like the goose which never quite laid the golden egg, the home market never fulfilled its promise to optical disc entrepreneurs until someone decided to use the technology to deliver high fidelity music. That move struck into the heart of a huge and lucrative market and the result so far has been a sensational success. Compact disc audio has wiped out the grim memories of the failed video disc market and has encouraged speculation about using compact discs in homes to provide forms of leisure other than listening to music. But can CD-ROM ever truly become a mass-market vehicle?

The only effort so far to tap the home market with CD-ROM has been Grolier's electronic encyclopaedia. At an initial price of $199, Grolier were offering customers access to each of their 30,000 encyclopaedia articles at about half a cent each! Clearly, Grolier faced a tough task selling the product, whatever its intrinsic merits, to a market that had no way of using the product. Without a single CD-ROM drive in American homes, their task was bound to be uphill. For a while, before publication, it looked as if Grolier would clinch a deal with Commodore who were interested in low-cost drives for their ST range of computers. The idea was to bundle the Grolier disc with the drives. But Commodore, lurching into financial crisis, dropped the idea and Grolier announced the disc without their support.

We have already referred to the electronic encyclopaedia several times and, indeed, it is hard to say much about CD-ROM initiatives without repeatedly mentioning it. Apart from its excellent and friendly design, it has the distinction of being CD-ROM's number one bestseller. With sales approaching 2500 copies and a new edition appearing shortly, it might look as if that goose had at last laid an egg for Grolier. However, much as the Grolier team deserve congratulation, it would be a serious mistake to infer from their achievement that a burgeoning home market exists for popular CD-ROM products. For one thing, Grolier's total revenues from sales must be well under half a million dollars so one suspects they are not yet making big profits. In addition, as Grolier freely admits, their biggest sales have been to other information publishers, keen to examine the first example of a mass-market CD-ROM. This factor in Grolier's sales success emphasises how much of the

CD-ROM industry is currently funding itself. So far there is little sign of the elusive 'end user' and in the main CD-ROM enthusiasts are doing the rounds trying to extract money from one another.

The real question is whether the *Electronic Encyclopaedia* proves anything about the home market potential for CD-ROM. Grolier's Peter Cook who masterminded the disc, thinks it was never likely to do so. Cook says, '. . . the disc is a part of a broader strategy as far as we are concerned. We'll not do too badly in American homes but the disc will be bought largely by real enthusiasts for the technology or by people who'll see it as a kind of status symbol. Certainly not by Mr Average in Middle America. We'll also do well with our Apple compatible version in US schools. But a real mass market has to wait for a multimedia disc technology where sound, pictures and text can be combined in a dynamic, interactive audio visual database. We believe that this is now a practical reality through compact disc interactive and we're already at work on a major CD-I project using the encyclopaedia as a basis.'

However, while Cook is surely right in believing that the mass market needs a multimedia product, Cook's view of CD-I may be overly optimistic. The launch of the first CD-I players has already been delayed and while many investors from the home entertainment industry are waiting in the wings for CD-I finally to appear, CD-ROM development seems to be rapidly overtaking CD-I in the race to create audio visual databases on CDs. For example, the Facts on File initiative, referred to earlier, has created the beginnings of a visual encyclopaedia on CD-ROM and clearly signals that some organisations are not waiting for CD-I. Increasingly image-handling techniques on CD-ROM are becoming hot news in the journals and newsletters of the optical disc industry. For the first time, the word 'multimedia' is frequently applied to CD-ROM. It was certainly never Philips' intention to encourage this development. Indeed their plans for a multimedia system were pinned firmly on CD-I. But they concede that CD-ROM is simply a hardware standard and, as such, is open to as much interpretation and development as human ingenuity will allow.

Despite this glimmer of hope for mass-market CD-ROMs, the likelihood remains that CD-I will be the real hope of the optical disc industry. CD-ROMs can undoubtedly be made to do most of the things CD-I discs will be able to do. In fact, this is hardly surprising since they are both effectively the same medium. But CD-ROM will fail because it will not fit into a home entertainment system without all the paraphernalia of special monitors and keyboards. CD-I is hitching its future to the meteoric rise of the compact disc music business. CD-ROM, for all the ingenuity of its proponents, will never be able to do this. It will always remain a specialised medium, never a mass-market one.

The best of the rest

In an area where niches abound, it would be easy to continue enumerating possible CD-ROM avenues until the list became wearisome. We ought however to touch upon two other markets where there may be lessons to be learned.

The first is document delivery. The electronic delivery of documents via on-line systems has been the subject of much research and debate for some years, especially in Europe where substantial Economic Community funds have been applied to a number of study exercises. What librarians and researchers, who are the principal customers for the documents, have indicated was that they did not need the speed of electronic delivery and certainly were not prepared to pay for it. Another experiment in the same area is a project called 'Adonis' which was set up by a consortium of publishers active in European markets with the aim of delivering journal articles to libraries using optical discs, and in this way preventing piracy of journals and magazines. Adonis has suffered several false starts and in late 1986 was having its third launch. Funding now seems agreed for an initial research and development phase centred on libraries such as the big medical library in Cologne, the Royal Academy of Science Library in Amsterdam and the British Library.

Adonis has also firmly decided on CD-ROM as the ideal optical delivery medium. The surprising feature of the project is that its demands on storage look as if they may stretch CD-ROM to its limits right from the start. Adonis has estimated that the 300 journals published annually by consortium members points to the need for a weekly CD-ROM containing the full text of some 1000 articles. Clearly, 52 discs each year will quickly build up to an unwieldy archive. As far as libraries are concerned they will have to look at the costs. Using CD-ROM may be cumbersome but it uses a standardised technology. Other optical disc storage such as video-disc-sized systems might accommodate the huge amount of data more comfortably but inevitably would be far more costly. The future of the project seems sure to hinge on this kind of trade-off between cost and convenience.

Library and bibliographic applications of CD-ROMs were the medium's first testing ground and most of the early disc products were in this general field. We need not give much time to examining the different projects which have been undertaken because none are really intended as money-making operations. The products are hardly likely to be the kind of generic material that most commercial information publishers are interested in.

In Britain a prototype of this kind of experimental project was mounted by the British Library. The aim of the initiative was purely evaluative and exploratory. The Library already offers a number of bibliographic databases on-line through its BLAISE-LINE service and it was keen to see whether CD-ROM might offer either a better alternative to on-line provision or a new added value information product for their customers. In the event, the British Library was also approached by Whitakers who publish *British Books in Print* (BBIP) and who were interested in replacing their monthly microfiche issues with CD-ROMs. The final experimental disc included three bibliographic files from BLAISE, 400,000 records from BBIP, a sample 107,000 records from the UK-MARC file and the 102,000 record Conference Proceedings index. The total database was about 200 megabytes.

The British Library disc is now being demonstrated very widely but it is not clear whether it has carried the British Library or anyone else very far forward. It may have taught them about some of the problems of making a CD-ROM but, as yet, has not resulted in clear feedback from end users. Indeed no systematic study of user response appears to have been made and the Library, in its recent report on the project, exudes satisfaction at the friendly responses to the disc expressed at an international book fair.

This type of project is clearly not motivated by the same commercial impulse familiar to most information publishers. Indeed the future plans of the Library confirm this, dominated as they are by further research in collaboration with universities and other academic centres. Quite clearly CD-ROMs have a natural application in libraries and few industry figures doubt that this is the first major area of use that will become commonplace. But it is not an environment that offers much promise to those seeking good commercial returns from generic products. Library and bibliographic databases look set to remain an interesting but insular testing ground for the technology while the real fortunes of the medium are won or lost elsewhere.

7

Compact Disc Evolution

We have already emphasised in an earlier chapter that evolution and revolution can often look alike. What makes evolution look like revolution is the pace of the change taking place. But revolution is much more than a rapid change. It carries an implication that an existing order is being overthrown. For example, when the White Russians gave way to the Red Russians in 1917, a way of life, a complete social, economic and political system was supplanted by a new one. Tsarist Russia was destroyed and the Soviet Union was born.

Fortunately revolutionary movements in the electronics industry are so far a lot less bloodthirsty. But they generate similar fears among colleagues and competitors in the industry. Will the old order be destroyed? Can the old and the new co-exist? Are important values from the old order being ignored? Will the new movement pull down the whole edifice and ruin everything for everyone? Alarm, despondency, defensiveness and eventually panic, take over from commonsense. And once an industry runs out of commonsense, it really is in danger of ruin.

All this is happening right now in the CD-ROM industry. Ironically the first bombshell came at the world's first big international conference on CD-ROM and, even more ironically, the people who exploded it were the very people who had given the world CD-ROM in the first place. The conference took place in 1986 in Seattle, organised by US giant Microsoft, and the people delivering the news that caused the confusion were the combined forces of Philips and Sony, who had earlier of course given us compact disc audio before CD-ROM. This time they caught everyone's attention by unveiling compact disc interactive (CD-I) and the vibrations are still travelling like a shockwave through the hearts and minds of CD-ROM protagonists all over the world. Curiously the commotion is being caused by a product that does not yet exist and which few people can fully specify. It remains an excellent example of 'vapourware' — a recent piece of jargon for high technology mirages.

More vapourware appeared a year later, at the same venue. Another major and unexpected unveiling revealed digital video interactive (DVI), a technology delivering the 'impossible': full-motion video on a CD-ROM. This time, at least, the insurrection did not come from the Philips/Sony axis. The culprits were General Electric and RCA.

What then is going on? Can an industry that is not yet really born, itself suffer a revolution? Is CD-ROM already under threat? To get the answers we need to look more closely at such initiatives as CD-I and DVI and see how they fit into the growing scheme of compact disc options. The picture we will get is one of considerable turmoil. However, the turmoil is caused more by misunderstanding than by genuine internecine threats. The reality has much more to do with evolution than with revolution.

What is compact disc interactive?

Before we deal with CD-I's role and rationale and its vexed relationship with CD-ROM, we need to specify what it offers. The following comes from Philips' own publication, *CD-I: the Compact Disc goes Interactive*.

> The key factor in CD-I, compared with the existing CD-ROM, is its ability to supplement the basic text and data information with visual material like still pictures, diagrams, high-quality computer graphics and cartoon-style animations, plus sound of every conceivable kind from top quality stereo to speech and sound effects, all simultaneously. In this new role, CD reaches maturity as a true multi-function, multi-purpose carrier for education, entertainment and information programme material. All the stored information can, if the user wishes, be accessed interactively — in other words, by means of a 'dialogue' procedure. Here the system presents the consumer with alternatives in a

friendly and 'human' manner, which he can then use to 'steer' his way to the desired information, using an exciting and entertaining procedure.

The full technical specification comes in yet another Philips/Sony 'colour' book, this time the so-called *Green Book*. Leaving the technicalities aside, however, we can see that CD-I is designed primarily as a multi-media product. More than this, it is a product that embodies the same transparency in its technology as a hi-fi music system. CD-I is a configuration both for discs and the hardware that plays them and crucial to its future is the fact that the hardware, the CD-I player, is really no more than a black box plugged into an ordinary television. No keyboards, no micro computer interfaces and no compatibility problems. All this is coupled to a product that delivers music, speech, sound effects, video-quality pictures, including full-motion animations, and the usual textual material we more commonly associate with CD-ROM. It is in a form that can be freely manipulated by the end user; in other words it is *interactive* information.

Philips themselves try to distinguish CD-ROM and CD-I by saying that CD-ROM is a software and data standard while CD-I is a 'system' standard. In other words, CD-I addresses the total package of disc and player. But this has not helped greatly and probably the best starting point in understanding the unique opportunity facing CD-I is the huge success scored by compact disc audio. It is, after all, the real beginning of the compact disc story. Millions of players and more millions of discs have been sold since its introduction in 1982. Increasingly, high-fidelity home stereo is being identified with compact disc technology. A mass consumer market has emerged and its swift growth has surprised even some of the most optimistic pundits. Yet many analysts believe that only the surface of the total market has been scratched. Most agree that well under ten per cent of the potential penetration of CD players has so far been achieved. This means that 150 million or more players will still be sold in the coming few years before we are near saturation and the market settles down to upgrades and replacements.

This huge potential market is important to the positioning strategy of CD-I. The key notion in CD-I is not the media facilities it offers but the way it is geared to the mass consumer market. After all, the features we used to describe CD-I — such as sound of different kinds, video images, text, animation, all delivered interactively — are not unique or even new. They are equalled and surpassed by the analogue laser video disc which has been available for years. The key difference is that home consumers failed to buy video disc players and no installed base hardware was ever established. The players suffered from the fact that they could only play video discs and nothing else. CD-I on the other hand relies on a player that will equally well play CD music. So the huge leisure market will shortly be buying CD-I as a component of an established entertainment product, already having tremendous popular success. At a stroke CD-I gets a vital and unique piggy-back into homes throughout the world. Even those who have already bought CD before CD-I becomes available will be able to upgrade easily to full CD-I capability. This means that CD-I can make the breakthrough into homes as a kind of added value hitched to the booming CD music business. Of course there will be an additional cost to consumers. The hardware will be more expensive than CD music players but many analysts expect that quite soon consumers will no more think of taking the cheaper option than they would think of buying a black and white television in preference to colour.

CD-I players

If the key to CD-I's future is the hardware, what will a CD-I player be like? Clearly, at the time of writing, it is difficult to say. Few people in the world have seen more than a working prototype. There are also some signs that Philips and Sony are encountering eleventh-hour problems because the launch of CD-I, once scheduled for 1987, has already been delayed for about a year. In fact the full Green Book specification was only released to hardware licencees and would-be CD-I disc developers in March 1987. There are, however, a few things we can be sure about.

So far, interactivity has always come from using computers. CD-I players, however, are emphatically not computers. At least, this is something about which the hardware manufacturers are very emphatic. The players may have a computer built in but, they point out, users will not need to know it. This way, the CD-I movement hopes to avoid the resistance home computers have faced. Despite their big sales, home computers have never become mass-market items like music systems and televisions. The reason is quite simple.

Most people dislike computers. They are hostile to the whole paraphernalia of keyboards, disc drives and dedicated monitors, not to mention the bewildering jungle of operating systems and memory configurations.

The CD-I 'non-computer' will house inside its casing micro processors of the Motorola 68000 family. The operating system, known as 'Compact Disc Real Time Operating System' (CD-RTOS) is based on the OS-9 system from Iowa-based Microware. The system is specially designed to handle switching in real time between the audio and video chips of the player.

The video outputs will be suitable both for the high resolution digital television standards soon to be commercially available and for existing worldwide television standards. Any disc produced to Green Book standards, wherever in the world it is made, will be playable on any CD-I machine, whether the machine's television output is NTSC, PAL or SECAM. All that must be matched is the television to the player. This means that the dream of all software publishers has finally come true. CD-I offers total worldwide compatibility for software.

The sound facilities allow for any or all of the following: digital audio quality, Hi-Fi music, 'Mid-Fi' (roughly FM broadcast quality), speech (AM broadcast quality) and synthesised speech quality. The output can either be played through the television or through high quality speakers. Either way, the CD-I player will require an amplifier in the same way as a conventional digital music player does.

One area of continuing uncertainty concerns the hardware that CD-I users will need to manipulate their CD-I discs. One of the key ideas, after all, is the interactivity of the medium. In order to interact, users need a convenient, friendly device that ideally can be used from the comfort of an armchair. What has been ruled out is a keyboard. That would inevitably evoke the spectre of the home computer. The likeliest option, therefore, is a remote-control handheld keypad or some infra-red pointing device.

Physically, the player will look much like a conventional CD audio machine. There is likely to be a switch with up to three positions: CD-A, CD-I and CD-ROM. So-called combi-players have also been displayed which can play both conventional analogue laser video discs and compact discs. Perhaps it is not too late after all for the ailing video disc industry to hitch its wagon to CD's rising star. Most digital disc watchers, however, dismiss the idea as implausible and regard the combi as a freakish hybrid.

The key question about CD-I players that no one is prepared to answer is, how much? At present there are a variety of views on what price tag the first CD-I players will carry. Philips and Sony are playing their cards close to their chest. But everyone knows that the price must be kept as low as possible if the dreams of major success are to be realised. The best estimates suggest that once the players are in reasonable volume production, the premium over a CD audio player will be about £150 in today's terms. By the early 1990s, when players are expected to be in mass production, the premium may disappear altogether.

CD-I discs

CD-I is really an integrated hardware and software standard so it is a little artificial to deal with discs separately. But most publishers will only be interested in players to the extent of knowing how many will be out in the market and that their discs will work on any of them. To them, the audio and video capabilities are disc-centred issues, opportunities to be used creatively in developing the software that ultimately will determine the fate of CD-I. The one lesson everyone has learned from the home computer bubble is that nothing sells hardware like software. Even if CD-I players are able to play music discs, there will be no market for even marginally more expensive players unless CD-I software is available to justify them.

The CD-I disc will look physically the same as a CD-ROM or an audio disc. However, it will be able to carry the different types of sound we have already described coupled to video quality images. Obviously, the quality of sound and vision encoded greatly affects the disc's capacity. For example, an ordinary audio compact disc can carry just over an hour of high quality stereo music. On a CD-I disc, if the only sound is normal speech, 16 hours of audio can be stored. In fact, if only minimal speech quality was required, similar to the reproduction of an average telephone, a continuous playing time of thousands of hours could be achieved. Similar rules apply to illustrations and animations on the disc. The more information required to convey them the more storage on the disc is consumed. For example, a line diagram can be stored using a few kilobytes of memory at most. One still colour picture of broadcast quality video, needs around 600 kilobytes. Using compression techniques available in CD-I, this can be reduced to 100 kilobytes so that about 7000 separate, top quality video pictures can be encoded in all.

Animation causes problems both of storage and data transfer. Animation of course relies on a series of images being displayed in rapid succession. Typically, in full-motion video, about 25 or 30 pictures each second have to be displayed in an appropriate sequence. If each is a full colour, broadcast quality picture, 2500 kilobytes per second of storage will be consumed. This would rock even the huge capacity of a CD-I disc. However, there is a more fundamental problem facing CD-I systems. Even if we were happy to use storage in this way, we still could not create full-motion video because we could not transfer each screen of data from disc to display fast enough. There is a basic constraint on the speed data can be pulled across to the television screen. Using the best compression techniques available in CD-I, it is possible to display three full screens every two seconds while audio is also playing. This is enough, for example, to illustrate a narrative or explain a technical sequence but a long way short of the requirements of full motion.

However, since the key is the speed of data transfer, there is a compromise solution. You cannot change the maximum rate at which data is transferred — that is fixed in the CD-I standard. But you can change the amount needed to refresh the screen and create the animation. One way of doing this is to animate images which can be described using much less data than natural video. For example, cartoon animation will work well on CD-I. Cartoon movie-makers have always known that the most economic way of creating an animation sequence is by only updating each picture by whatever it is that changes and no more. In other words, do not constantly redraw backgrounds or other features that do not move from frame to frame. Only redraw what changes — a hand, a leg or an expression, for example. In CD-I we can apply the same approach by storing on the disc only what changes in a sequence, frame to frame. This, coupled with other compression techniques, reduces the overall storage requirement and, more important, dramatically cuts the amount of data that has to be transferred to the television display to refresh the screen and create the animated effect. So while CD-I cannot deliver normal full-motion video, it can certainly offer animated cartoon graphics.

However, it is unfair to say absolutely that CD-I cannot deliver full-motion video. It can, but not on all the screen at once. Obviously, if the key problem is that the whole display screen cannot be refreshed quickly enough to create full motion, then only refresh one small part of the screen. This means that you can have full-motion video so long as it is not also 'full screen' video. Typically a small box on the screen can contain some full motion while, perhaps, the rest of the screen shows a static graphic image with a voice-over providing an audio complement. For example, on a natural history disc, you may choose to show the distribution of zebra in Africa with a colour map, explaining the information through the voice-over while illustrating a running herd of zebra in a box in one section of the screen. The technique works well as a means of bringing life to an otherwise static display.

In addition to sound and vision, the CD-I disc can also store computer data and computer programs which of course would be essential to a fully interactive use of the medium. In other words, the control software enabling users to search and retrieve specific data or to experience the sense of control over a character in an interactive CD drama, will be built into the disc. No separate floppy disc will be needed nor will there be a means of using it. The essence of CD-I is its appearance to the end user of total simplicity.

CD-I products

It is too early to foresee exactly what the line-up of CD-I products will be when Philips/Sony finally launch their systems. At the time of writing, best estimates suggest there will be a catalogue of about 50 CD-I discs by late 1988. Whether all the discs will actually be available by that time, however, is far from clear.

Although we cannot specify the products in detail, one thing is sure. They will be geared to a mass consumer market and the emphasis will be on leisure and entertainment. This is fundamental to the whole concept of CD-I. Investors are looking to the full flowering of that mass market by the early 1990s and then they are looking for sales of individual disc titles of hundreds of thousands. In other words, CD-I is being seen as a direct analogue of the music business. CD-I disc prices will be about twice their audio counterparts, probably starting at around $29.95. Some more specialised discs such as encyclopaedias, will probably retail for about $100.

Philips have seen from the outset that the CD-I initiative stands or falls on the discs available. Even if their hardware can always play any of the existing audio discs, they still have to demonstrate the added value of CD-I with a range of excellent CD-I products available on the high street. To try to make sure the right CD-I projects get under way, Philips have formed a joint venture with the PolyGram Corporation to establish American Interactive Media (AIM). In the United States, AIM is stimulating disc development by liaising with market leaders in diverse areas — entertainment, personal computing, publishing and education — in order to convince them to make CD-I commitments. AIM's work includes offering funding arrangements where necessary. Gordon Stulberg, AIM's chief executive, says, 'AIM's mission is to establish joint venture relationships with companies that will provide software for the CD-I system. Through the auspices of Philips and PolyGram and with a highly knowledgeable staff . . . AIM is well qualified to offer technical expertise and access to production and distribution channels'.

Other Philips/PolyGram organisations are being established in other parts of the world. In Europe in late 1986, for example, European Interactive Media was unveiled. Like its American parent, EIM is also looking for joint venture partners. From its base in London, EIM's president, Byron Turner, is looking for organisations prepared to help make the right kind of products. When asked who he was talking to in Europe, Turner explained, 'I'm not going to name names yet. . . . But a key group for us is publishers. They seem to understand interactive media better than others — and they certainly have suitable material from their print titles.' There seems little question of allowing American generated products to dominate the European markets. Turner says, 'If we can bring some over successfully — great. But only 25 to 40 per cent of American software is successful or relevant in Europe. We have to come up with that missing percentage here in Europe in order to have a proper catalogue.'

It is already possible to get a flavour of some of the products either in development or planned. In the United States, The Record Group, funded by Philips to produce original CD-I programming, is already describing some of its first discs. Stan Cornyn who runs The Record Group is also a senior vice president of Warner Communications, so he understands the mass market entertainment business and is determined to make CD-I succeed in that same arena. The four discs Cornyn recently unveiled include something for almost everyone. *London: Anyway You Turn* is a kind of surrogate travel experience enabling you to take a 'walk' through London, experiencing the city by both sight and sound. You can choose where you go and whether you turn right or left. The interactive disc keeps up with your decisions. But the disc also enables you to travel back in time. You can experience London in eight different eras including the time of Shakespeare and the time of Chaucer.

Continuing the theme of time travel, another Record Group disc is called *The Time Machine*. The disc is planned to trace the history of civilisation from 700 BC to the present day. In a different vein, a group of writers and actors have been brought together with a computer games designer, to produce a disc called *Danger in Dreamland*. The idea is to create a fully interactive audio visual game. Cornyn says, 'I call it interactive fiction. It's like going to a movie with a steering wheel.'

The fourth of the Record Group's projects may have a clear message for print-based publishers. Currently untitled, the planned disc is a huge encyclopaedic reference work on classical music. Using thousands of illustrations, hours of musical and other audio material, Cornyn expects the disc to provide a lively and popular resource.

At least one publisher is already taking the point and is trying to make another kind of encyclopaedia 'come alive'. We have already examined Grolier's electronic exploitations of their *Academic American Encyclopaedia*. Now they are working on a further development — a CD-I version. Grolier's brief and unhappy experience of trying to develop a consumer-level video disc encyclopaedia gave them two advantages. It gave them direct experience working with interactive audio visual material and it linked them to an energetic and creative team based in London and run by Dick Fletcher, known as New Media. Today, with the memories of the defunct video disc project behind them, Grolier and New Media are hard at work on a major CD-I development.

The Grolier/New Media disc will embody ten million words, over 4000 pictures, animations, three or four hours of audio — both music and narration — and part-screen full-motion video. Grolier's experience of optical discs shows very clearly in what they say about the disc. Peter Cook who runs the CD-I project for Grolier, made an important statement of CD-I values when he spoke at an optical disc conference in Amsterdam in April 1987:

> The home TV imposes very real technical limitations, such as the low resolution text display. And it also imposes certain expectations. Because most TV viewers have at least a subliminal sense of the high production values of broadcast TV programmes, our product cannot look like a home movie by comparison. And for the same reason, the encyclopaedia must have seamless transitions — no screen blanking, slow screen refresh or lengthy delays as the drive thrashes around trying to keep up with the user. And the user — let's not forget him or her — could be an 8 year old child or a 60 year old adult because the potential audience for our Multimedia Encyclopaedia spans a vast range of ages and experience. For that reason, simple ease of use is essential — no complex commands, no keyboard requirement. . . . The encyclopaedia has not been designed primarily as a home reference tool — though it can fulfill that function — rather it has been designed to intrigue, stimulate, encourage curiosity, provide a rich vehicle for open ended exploration of a multi-faceted database. We have done this by surrounding the text with a number of different modules: audio visual essays, picture banks, games and something we call 'The Time Machine'. All these modules are linked to each other and to the text. . . . We are busy producing this product right now.

Cook anticipates a price of $99 for his CD-I encyclopaedia and expects to sell well over 300,000 copies.

CD-I and CD-ROM

With some picture of CD-I in our minds, we can begin to get a view of its relationship with CD-ROM.

The role of CD-I is straightforward enough. It is a mass-market consumer product. It will concentrate on leisure and entertainment and discs will be low price, high volume products. Distribution will probably be largely through high street outlets, multiples and independents, including record, leisure electronics and computer software stores. It is also possible that CD-I will provide the basis of educational and training products. For example, it would be an ideal vehicle for language teaching in schools, colleges and homes.

What then of CD-ROM? Does CD-I supersede it or even offer a threat? Were Philips and Sony killing off their own fledgling by introducing the newcomer? The answer is clear. CD-I does nothing to outmode CD-ROM. This is to misunderstand both media. CD-I could not exist without CD-ROM. In fact, it is no more than a special use of the CD-ROM medium. If we imagine CD-ROM as the trunk of the optical disc tree, CD-I is an applications-specific branch growing from the main body. The particular applications are consumer entertainment, education and training.

There are also many important contrasts between CD-I and CD-ROM. One is obvious. CD-ROM is available right now. CD-I is still a total newcomer. This has some immediate implications. At a development level, authoring techniques and utilities are already available for CD-ROM while they are in their infancy for CD-I. Moreover CD-I is an inherently costly medium, including as it does, sound, text, graphics and animation. CD-ROM is mostly used in text-only applications and offers excellent opportunities to move more or less directly from a print product to a CD-ROM counterpart. This all means that while hundreds of thousands of pounds may be needed to create a full-facility CD-I product, a CD-ROM product can be produced for tens of thousands. This may not matter to overall profitability. Pricing and volume sales will decide that issue. But it fundamentally affects the degree of commercial commitment demanded of potential disc publishers. Going into CD-I means putting a great deal of money on the table. It is a big gamble for big stakes.

Another contrast is the requirement on external computing resources. CD-I has none and, with an onboard Motorola 68000 processor, it is hardly likely that it could be adapted to become any kind of peripheral to IBM PC environments since these rely on Intel processors. The CD-ROM, however, is conceived as a peripheral to a computer and with the emergence of new device driver software, is compatible with a wide range of modern desktop work stations. This emphasises that the principal area of application is in the business, research/academic and library environments.

We are left with two related but different media, each appropriate to different applications. CD-I may well flourish in the home where pictures, animation and stereo sound are important. But many commercial and other applications simply do not need these facilities and neither would people want to give up the storage facility on the disc in order to have them. CD-ROM is here for the long term. It is not dependent on a particular computer processor or operating system like CD-I and can therefore survive generations of change in computer systems. CD-I may have a good future ahead of it but it is ultimately ephemeral. Like most consumer products it will be replaced or evolve into new vehicles to deliver the raw material of leisure and entertainment into the home.

Perhaps most interesting of all — and most threatening to proponents of CD-I — is the flexibility of CD-ROM. We have already seen that inventive and technically innovative teams can work within the CD-ROM standard to create audio visual products well before the first CD-I disc has seen the light of day. Indeed, the CD-ROM standard is in no way a set of limitations. It is, by contrast, a basis for development, a springboard for future new products. With publications like the Facts on File visual encyclopaedia already well advanced, some industry commentators suggest that if CD-I suffers many more delays, CD-ROM innovation will have cut the ground from under it by offering the same kind of facilities.

However, this misses an important point. Even if CD-ROM replicates exactly the capabilities of CD-I, even if it improves upon them, it is not primarily configured to be a successful mass-market product. CD-I has, locked into its specification, the key to huge consumer success. The acceptability of the hardware in homes as a natural extension of commonplace music systems gives CD-I a crucial advantage over any other similar competing technology. CD-ROM remains a powerful computer peripheral, valuable wherever computer technology is happily accepted. The home is definitely not one of those places. The workplace, for example, is.

Ultimately we are not seeing an attempted coup. CD-I was never intended to overthrow CD-ROM nor could it hope to do so. In terms of the markets they address, the two systems are complementary. The arguments and debates that seek to emphasise conflict between CD-I and CD-ROM are a misdirection of effort.

CD-V and DVI

We are not out of the acronym jungle yet! Two more have recently emerged which represent unexpected developments that have confused CD-I/CD-ROM arguments still further.

While CD-I delays were being announced by one part of the Philips/Sony organisation, another was announcing an unexpected new product called Compact Disc Video (CD-V). Ready for launch in 1987, a year ahead of CD-I, the new system is based on the mass-market compact disc audio philosophy. This time however, the disc provides a combination of four or five minutes of analogue full-motion video and about forty minutes of digital sound. The most obvious application will be for music discs that combine some video 'footage' to accompany and enhance the sound. Philips claim that CD-V players will also play both CD-A and CD-I discs. Upward compatibility, they say, is crucial to the strategy.

So far, few people know what to make of the sudden unveiling of CD-V. There is serious speculation as to whether it is a deliberate attempt to upstage CD-I which is beginning to suffer frustrating launch delays. Whatever the reality of this, a cool appraisal of CD-V certainly suggests it cannot challenge the kind of product CD-I is capable of delivering. CD-V looks like a perfectly agreeable 'musical juke box' that could do well in the same way that pop music videotapes do well in the VCR market. It is nothing more.

Digital Video Interactive (DVI) is much more interesting. After CD-I was unveiled at Microsoft's first CD-ROM conference in Seattle in 1986, the people attending the second in March 1987 must have been reminded of the slogan that advertised the Jaws movie: '. . . just when you thought it was safe to go back in the water'! This time General Electric and RCA shook the conference with an hour of full-screen, full-motion video on a standard CD-ROM disc.

DVI is essentially an ingenious compression-decompression system for digital video and audio information. On American televisions, full-motion video demands thirty frames per second and this implies, on a compact disc, the transfer of nearly 18 million bytes of data per second from disc to display. DVI compression reduces this to around 150,000 bytes per second.

The system has been developed secretly in a Princeton laboratory over the past three years and RCA were ready with a number of excellent demonstrations at the Seattle conference. However, the excitement of the technological breakthrough must have intoxicated most observers because little attention was paid at the time to the applications and commercial potential of the new system. The *New York Times* correspondent wrote that DVI 'could mean the death of the CD-I system'. For those who attended the first

CD-ROM conference and saw the unveiling of CD-I, it must have seemed a strange irony.

But is DVI a real threat to CD-I and where exactly does it fit into the fast growing compact disc mosaic? An important factor is the special DVI chip, central to the system. The chip performs the vital data decompression needed to construct the video frames. It also allows text and graphics to be combined with full-motion video and the whole DVI system to be interfaced with a range of personal computers. Initial estimates suggest the first prototype chip will be available at the end of 1987 for the IBM AT at a price of several thousand dollars. General Electric and RCA believe that the price can be reduced to a level acceptable to home applications within three years. The DVI chip is really the heart of DVI. While CD-ROM and CD-I are agreed standards, DVI remains a proprietary piece of hardware that can be integrated into the architecture of any system with which it is compatible. In this sense, DVI looks much more like an adjunct to CD-ROM or CD-I rather than a replacement. For example, we could easily imagine DVI as a kind of CD-ROM peripheral, allowing full-motion video to be added to the other features of CD-ROM.

But whether or not DVI is destined to remain a peripheral to other systems, it puts pressure on CD-I and, in particular, re-opens the argument about the adequacy of CD-I's video capabilities. The real question being asked is 'how important is full-motion video in a multimedia consumer product'? Philips argue that CD-I does all it needs to do right now. Others say that DVI emphasises the shortcomings of CD-I and will serve to accelerate the research almost certainly being carried out by Philips to create full-screen full-motion video within the CD-I standard.

Clearly DVI has a long way to go. There is little doubt that DVI picture quality is not as good as the CD-I criterion. This is generally regarded as crucial to consumer acceptance so on this issue alone, DVI has to improve its performance. In addition, DVI costs will take years to get down to levels acceptable to consumers. At present, it is impossible to know what the final price level will be and, even if ultimately it looks attractive, CD-I may by that time have trumped the RCA ace with an expanded CD-I capability.

However, it is too early to talk in terms of a conflict between DVI and CD-I. General Electric executives at Seattle admitted that they had no business plan to accompany their technological marvel.

They now have to decide what to do with it. When they have finished their deliberations we may see DVI tackling the business and professional market as a CD-ROM add-on rather than setting up as a rival to CD-I. The only danger to CD-I then would be if Philips/Sony continue to bungle their launch dates. If they take too long to get CD-I into the market, consumer CD-ROMs might start to make impact, pulling DVI along with them.

8

Publishing Options

When a conventional print publisher reviews a new information medium such as optical discs, he can be forgiven a sigh of relief. Thank goodness he is involved with books! By contrast with optical discs, books offer well-trodden, predictable territory. The technology behind manufacturing books is familiar, the market forces that shape demand are understood and the medium is stable and reliable. Books have little to prove. They have withstood the test of centuries and even today cock a snook at the up and coming technologies by being the medium through which the newcomers themselves are debated. Many of today's publishers can rightly call themselves 'new technology' publishers because they publish so many excellent and saleable books on the subject! Who can blame a publisher familiar with product life cycles of three, five, even ten years being dismissive or simply uncomprehending when faced with the helter-skelter of change commonplace in electronic media. To the conventional publisher, technology-based products look like a fast and ever-moving target. Why bother even to risk a single shot?

There is little doubt that the new technologies are fast moving. But all motion is relative. A runner looks as if he is moving quickly as he jogs past you. But that is only because you are standing still. If you jog alongside, he might as well be motionless. If you run faster, he will seem to go backwards. The moral is that technology-based publishing is only full of difficult moving targets if you yourself are stationary. Conventional publishers have to leave the comfort of familiar business methods and get on the move if they are to stand a chance of making sense of the future of their business.

Why bother?

Is it worthwhile to make the effort and pay the price of finding out about electronic media? Does it pass the 'so what test'?

Publishers are sometimes characterised as business people who lack a cutting edge and a sense of vision about the future. Like many generalisations, it is unfair but contains a grain of truth. There has always been an understandable complacency in book publishing about the current value and secure future of books, journals and magazines; the so-called paper media. Picture a modern international publisher who can cast his eyes over thriving lists, healthy subsidiary rights accounts and consign technology to the care of his production managers: they will know how to use it to save money on manufacturing outlays by choosing the most up-to-date typesetting, printing and binding processes. We have already rehearsed two key arguments for taking new media publishing seriously. First, it may represent a threat to our established markets so we had better take steps to know the enemy. Second, it may offer new business opportunities, perhaps complementing our existing publishing. Our contented international publisher who has little to do but consider the profitability of his existing business might well say, '. . . if there's a threat, I can see no sign of it. If it's an opportunity, why do I need it? There's no opportunity without some cost and some risk, so why should I bother?'

Our contented international publisher is, of course, fictional: no publisher would survive if he was so smug and self-satisfied. The message is simple. If you have a business that is so comfortable in its profitability that you need no new avenues for expansion or diversification or if you have a business that is secure from all threats of changes in market conditions, you can safely forget all about the new media. But if you do not have that kind of business, you need to bother with them. Wherever the new media may ultimately lead, you need to move with them, acquiring knowledge, experience and the readiness to take advantage of real opportunities the moment they mature.

Degrees of commitment

In any field of business, you need to take a balanced view of the risks you are willing to run. Publishing, like any other business, has a strong element of gambling in its make-up. This does not mean that publishers take wild risks. Gambling is about risk strategies not foolhardy gestures. Certainly, chance plays a part in the outcomes but most serious gamblers will say they make their own luck. So do publishers. Just as a poker player will win more times than he loses if he understands the probabilities governing his chosen game, so publishers will make money if they play their game consistently with the right combination of flair and professionalism.

The extent of the risk you are prepared to take is ultimately a question of cash. But financial commitment has to be measured in both direct and indirect terms. Straight investment is, on the whole, easily accounted for although how returns may be required on it is a complex sub-issue to which we need to return. Overhead can also be apportioned by a common sense formula. Opportunity cost, however, presents a much greater problem.

Opportunity cost is the price a business pays for doing one thing when it could be doing another. If you spend an hour of your time fixing a deal earning your company £1000 when you could have spent that same hour fixing another earning the same, the opportunity cost is £1000. You traded the opportunity to do one deal against the opportunity to do another because you could not do two things at the same time. Of course, if you would otherwise have spent the hour non-productively, the opportunity cost is zero. This kind of mathematics is easy. However, the real life situation is rarely so straightforward. Most of the time, we do not know exactly what we could have been achieving with our time. Clearly, there are times when someone spends an hour earning £1000 when the time could obviously have been spent securing a deal worth much more. Leaving aside the issue of opportunity cost, this is just bad management and bad judgement, easily detectable at this kind of individual level. But how do you evaluate a new corporate initiative? To what degree does such an initiative inhibit or prevent other business opportunities being scooped up? How is it possible to decide what, if any, productive opportunity is slipping past?

There are no sure formulas to work this out. Certain situations are easier to assess than others. But the essential point to remember is that opportunity cost cannot be ignored. A view must be taken, especially when a company is considering moving into such uncertain areas as electronic publishing.

Determining the degree of commitment you are prepared to

make is a matter of balancing risk against return. In a more straightforward publishing context, this is purely a matter of commercial arithmetic. You can prepare budgets and forecast likely outcomes from a new operation, applying varying contingencies to reflect the risk outlooks you wish to adopt. The profitability and the return on investment together with any other business ratios you wish to apply, give you a clear, quantitative view of your prospects. Clearly, many subjective judgements form a part of such a business plan but there remains a solid bedrock of objectivity which provides some grounds for taking the commercial projections seriously.

A CD-ROM initiative or a similar push into new media publishing, is a significantly different situation. There is no doubt that you can contrive a business plan. It can even look convincingly quantitative. But the reality, if you are prepared to face it, is one largely of conjecture and guesswork. We have already indicated that market information exists; some competitive products are available to assess; there is both an industry track record of sorts and no shortage of projections about the future. If you are careful, you can make reliable estimates of the direct cost of developing and manufacturing products. The real problem is deciding how believable all the information really is. We are dealing with media which are so new that the markets for them are embryonic. How will they evolve and will they flourish or only briefly flare before dwindling to nothing? Ultimately, even armed with as much firm information as is available, it is still anybody's guess.

So there is an inherent and massive uncertainty factor that cannot be avoided. The important thing is to be aware of it. Produce business plans by all means but recognise that they are, at best, an educated stab in the dark. Beyond this, there are further problems. The commercial returns shown in your business plan are, leaving aside their dubious accuracy, only a part of the picture. The rest depends on your corporate objectives for taking the initiative in the first place. It brings us back to the 'why bother' question. The answer must always involve a large element of research and development. Of course one hopes to do some successful publishing but no one can sensibly believe CD-ROM or something similar is a short-term money spinner. It may become one if the market develops in the right way but it may also lead to nothing but disappointment. This means that an important part of your assessment of commercial returns lies in a growing knowledge of a new medium and in the fact that you will be well placed to take advantage of market opportunities should they emerge.

It is something of a magical mystery tour because, even if you start as a would-be CD-ROM publisher, you may find yourself ultimately making money in a different product area altogether. Exploring optical disc technology brings you in touch with a world of high technology products. You find yourself in a territory with a number of roads to travel. And new roads are being built all the time. To make the utmost of the research and development ingredient of your commitment, you need to maintain a flexible, open-minded attitude to the future paths your initiative may take.

We have said that determining your degree of commitment is a question of balance. The real problem is that since you have no way of knowing what your return may be, you cannot balance your commitment against it. The best you can do is to take a view on that return and be guided by it. In the end it is an individual or corporate judgement.

There is of course a practical issue here too. Minimal commitment, standing on the touchlines and doing little else, can only give you a very general feel for the game being played. It may be an easy option but it will not provide you with anything of much value. You probably need to get onto the field. In other words, commitment confined purely to reading the literature, treading the conference and symposium circuits and looking at the competition, may never give you enough knowledge to even justify the low level of cost incurred. It may be ultimately a waste of time or, at best, a token gesture towards 'keeping up with the times'. To acquire real insights you will need to dirty your hands and make some investments. Product development, even at a modest and cautious level, is dramatically more fruitful than any amount of watching and listening. The key lies in the disciplines you apply to your chosen initiative. A controlled experiment which carries you into a new field at a measured pace is probably the best middle ground between enthusiastic overcommitment and timorous toe-dipping exercises.

The controlled Experiment

The key factors in a successful controlled Experiment are: planning, staffing, monitoring and backing.

You must have a business plan with all the usual budgetary

provisions and timescales plus a clear statement of philosphy. What is the initiative trying to achieve? Is it a CD-ROM exploration pure and simple? Or is there a much broader canvas? Is the company riding the electronic publishing roller-coaster to see where it goes with an open mind about the possible destination?

You need to have the right kind of staff and you will have to decide whether they are to be dedicated exclusively to the Experiment or whether they will also do more orthodox publishing jobs at the same time. What you get out of the Experiment is who you put into it. The team need not be large. Much can be achieved with two or three able and highly-motivated pragmatists. But they will have to be energetic, entrepreneurial and ready to accept the stress of entering an environment where the rules and frameworks are as yet unclear. Business start-ups of any kind are tough undertakings and an Experiment of this type is no exception. The chosen team must also be strongly commercial in outlook. There is always the danger of selecting enthusiasts for the technology. They are the people most likely to seek the job and be most immediately prepared to take it on. What is really needed is a more hard-headed commercial attitude that can look dispassionately on the technologies, seeing them simply as delivery systems for information products. You need good publishers not technology buffs.

Once the Experiment is under way, you must be able to monitor its activity. The emphasis must be on controlling the Experiment at all stages. This does not mean tampering with those constraints already built into the original business plan. It just means knowing what the Experiment is costing and what returns are accruing. Reporting systems agreed with the key staff are vital both to ensure that the measured pace of the initiative is neither grinding to a halt nor accelerating into a mad gallop, and to maintain the team's sense of accountability. Without accountability, there is no drive to succeed and no sense of recognition of the successes achieved. You may need to cost the operation on a marginal basis. In other words, depending on the circumstances, it may be unreasonable to expect the Experiment to recover all its overheads if large elements would have to be paid whether or not the Experiment was in progress. The best approach is to construct two monitoring frameworks. In one, the performance of the Experiment is regarded as just another corporate profit centre. In the other 'hidden' framework, full allowance is made by top management for the marginality of costs and for the intangible returns that should be accruing whatever the bottom line says.

Finally, the Experiment needs the right management backing. It must not be simply the brainchild and enthusiasm of one manager, however senior. It needs the genuine, consistent backing of the top figures in the organisation and that backing must not be fudged. It has to be clearly stated and it has to be real.

CD-ROM and beyond

This book has been primarily about CD-ROM. However, we have tried to maintain a broader perspective. No publisher interested in new electronic media can afford to be blinkered. It is vital to see any one avenue in its context amongst others. Whether through a controlled experiment of the kind just described or through a more extensive commitment of resources, a publisher needs to retain flexibility. CD-ROM may be an end in itself or it may be no more than a beginning. Imagine yourself back in the closing years of the fifteenth century. Johannes Gutenberg has just invented the movable type printing press. What would you have made of the implications of the invention? Would you have realised that the world was on the brink of a unique revolution that would change the lives of millions? Trying to assess the future of CD-ROM and other optical disc media is like trying to evaluate the book publishing industry fifty years after Gutenberg.

It is essential not to become locked into any particular delivery system whether it is based on paper, computer tapes or compact discs. Publishers succeed ultimately because they are good business people and because they combine with their professionalism, a freedom of vision; a creative facility that examines a variety of avenues with the single objective of getting an information product to its market effectively, efficiently and profitably.

Peter Cook of Grolier sums it up for us:

> We take a very pragmatic view of optical disc technologies. Frankly, we couldn't care less how the technology is labelled as long as it works, is easy to use and can bring value to our products at the right price. Grolier is a publisher. Our business is selling information-based products to a broad general audience. Yes, we are enthusiastic about the current developments in optical

disc technology . . . as long as these technologies can ultimately give us the volume of sales required to build a substantial long-term business. For us that's the bottom line.

Glossary

The following glossary is by no means comprehensive and is intended as a brief and selective aid for readers of this book who have no technical or computing experience.

AIM Stands for American Interactive Media, a Philips/PolyGram subsidiary company based in Los Angeles. Its objective is to stimulate **CD-I** developments in the United States.

analogue information Information conveyed by a continuously varying value. A conventional (ie non-digital) wrist-watch is a good example of an analogue display. The time is indicated by the relationship between two continuously moving pointers.

applications software Computer programs which fulfill specific uses for end users. Such software includes word processing, spreadsheet and database packages.

bit The basic unit of machine readable information from which all such information is built up. In computer technology, a bit corresponds to a binary digit, either 1 or 0, and all computer information consists of sequences of these two digits.

bit error rate A measure of how well a medium such as **CD-ROM** can store and transmit data without errors. It is generally expressed as the number of **bits** the medium can transmit with only one error.

byte The smallest unit of addressable information that can be stored in a computer, generally eight **bits** long. The word in fact is a contraction of 'by eight'.

CAV Stands for Constant Angular Velocity. A way of rotating an optical disc in its player so that the disc always turns at the same speed as the laser stylus moves over its surface. CAV is one of the two modes used in Philips' **LaserVision** video disc system. The other is Constant Linear Velocity (**CLV**).

CD-A Stands for compact disc audio.

CD-I Stands for compact disc interactive.

CD-ROM Stands for compact disc read only memory.

CD-V Stands for compact disc video.

CIRC Stands for Cross-Interleaved Reed-Solomon Code. A system enabling compact disc players to detect and correct bit errors.

CLV Stands for Constant Linear Velocity. A way of rotating an optical disc so that the disc rotates at a varying speed as the laser stylus tracks across the surface of the disc. This variation keeps the linear speed, at which the stylus reads any track, constant. The disc spins more quickly when the outer tracks are being read and slows for the inner tracks which are of course shorter in length. This system maximises playing time but makes rapid addressing of particular tracks difficult. Used in non-interactive **LaserVision** video discs and in all compact discs. Compare **CAV.**

connect time Usually applied to the time a user of an **on-line database** remains connected by telephone or other communication link to the computer hosting the **database.**

database A large accumulation of data. The contents of a library could be a database as could the contents of a telephone directory. Widely used to mean a massive body of data held electronically.

digital information Information consisting of discrete, individual 'packets' of data that together build up to form a message. This is the kind of information that modern computers handle. In computers the digital data is stored, processed and transferred in the form of binary code, a sequence of 1s and 0s. The basic unit of information (the information 'packet') is called a **bit.**

DVI Stands for digital video interactive.

EIM AIM's counterpart in Europe. Based in London and working to stimulate European **CD-I** initiatives.

electronic publishing The term has two usages. It can mean the application of modern electronic technology to print production processes. Perhaps the best example of this is the so-called desktop publishing system. It can also mean the development of information products which are themselves electronic. This includes videotapes, computer software, **on-line databases** and **CD-ROM**s. It is important always to define very clearly in which sense the term is being used.

error detection and correction codes Established electronic systems designed to detect and correct flaws in the **bits** of **digital information.** The most rigorous systems are used in **CD-ROM** and **CD-I** applications, based on the **Cross-Interleaved Reed-Solomon Code** first developed for compact disc audio.

gigabyte A unit of data of one thousand million **bytes.**

Green Book The informal name given to the Philips/Sony specification of **CD-I.**

header A part of a data sector of a **CD-ROM** or **CD-I** disc containing the sector's electronic address.

High Sierra Group An ad hoc group set up in 1985 to recommend standards for **CD-ROM.** It was named after the hotel in which the group first met.

interactive Any system is interactive if it can respond and change in accordance with external inputs or stimuli. A data system, such as an optical disc, is interactive if a user can determine his own path through the data. The high street arcade game uses an interactive video disc under computer control. The user can 'participate' in a cartoon adventure, taking decisions on the actions of the hero and changing the course of the adventure.

inversion In the preparation of databases, inverting files means a form of detailed indexing so that subsequent searches of the **database** can be made very quickly by reference to an index file rather than repeated searches of the entire database. Applications software packages exist to handle the inversion process but even with computer assistance it can be a lengthy and therefore costly process.

laser A device which stores energy and releases it as a beam of intense, pure light. The beam can be very precisely focused and is used as a 'stylus' to read the information encoded on digital optical discs.

LaserVision Philips' optical video disc system. As with compact discs the information is read by a laser stylus but, in contrast to the digital format of compact discs, the information is encoded in an analogue form.

log-on/log-off The protocols required respectively to connect and disconnect, via a computer, modem and telephone or other communication link, to an **on-line database** system or similar. They generally involve a sequence of keyboard entries although software is now available to handle the log-on procedures automatically.

on-line database A **database** held as files on a mainframe computer and distributed to the user 'on-line' through telecommunication links.

off-line database A **database** which can be interrogated directly by the end user without, for example, the need for telecommunications links to connect them 'on-line' with a distant computer. A **CD-ROM** is a good example of an off-line database. So is a book.

random access memory (RAM) An electronic memory which can both be written into and read. 'Random access' means information can be extracted in any order and from any location in the memory.

read only memory (ROM) An electronic memory which can be read but not altered.

search software Sometimes called 'search and retrieval' or just 'retrieval software'. **Applications software** that enables the user to search through a large electronic **database** and locate and retrieve the required information.

sector The smallest unit of addressable information in a **CD-ROM** or **CD-I** disc. Typically a sector consists of 2352 **bytes** of data. Part will consist of technical information about the sector such as its address, **header** and **synchronisation** pattern.

synchronisation The first 12 **bytes** of a **CD-ROM** or **CD-I** sector containing information controlling the timing and coordination of the various processes required to get information off the disc.

WORM Stands for Write Once Read Many and refers to a type of digital optical disc system that allows users to write their own data on a disc. The data, once written, cannot be altered.

Yellow Book The informal name for the Philips/Sony **CD-ROM** specification.

Further Reading

There is a large and burgeoning literature of CD-ROM and optical disc technology in general. The following short list of suggested further reading is therefore by no means exhaustive, Neither is it necessarily a list of the best so authors whose works are excluded should not feel slighted. It should, however, help readers who wish to explore more fully the field of optical disc publishing.

Journals

CD-I News, published monthly by Link Resources Corporation, 79 Fifth Avenue, New York, NY 10003, USA. An excellent, chatty newsletter that invariably contains a few surprises and a few new insights into the hurly-burly of CD-I. Anyone the slightest bit interested in this medium should subscribe.

CD-ROM Review, published by CW Communications/Peterborough Inc, Elm Street, Peterborough, New Hampshire, USA. First published in October 1986, *CD-ROM Review* is a brash and cheerful mixture of 'Readers Digest' style and more serious articles on CD-ROM and CD-I. The quality of the articles varies and the journal seems a little partisan in its approach to optical disc publishing, but it is an interesting and useful read. Obviously very USA orientated. But who isn't?

Electronic and Optical Publishing Review, published monthly by Learned Information Europe Limited, Woodside, Hinksey Hill, Oxford, England. An international review of the optical disc scene aimed at the serious reader. The articles and general coverage are often fairly technical. Excellent news and bibliography sections.

Monitor, published monthly by Learned Information Europe Limited. Described by the publishers as 'an analytical review of current events in electronic information', *Monitor* has in the past dealt largely with the on-line database industry. Increasingly it now includes articles on optical disc publishing. It has a refreshingly commonsense approach to the subject and offers pungent criticism of aspects of the electronic publishing world that most deserve it.

Books and booklets

The following from Philips are a must:

A General Introduction to CD-Interactive
CD-I: The Compact Disc goes interactive
Philips in the Age of Optical Disc Media

Published by New Media Information Centre, Philips International B.V., Building HWD, PO Box 218, 5600 MD Eindhoven, The Netherlands.

Other important reading includes the following:

CD-ROM: The New Papyrus, edited by Steve Lambert and Suzanne Ropiequet; published by Microsoft Press, 16011 NE 36th Way, Box 97017, Redmond, Washington 98073-9717, USA. The original 'seminal' work.

CD-ROM Volume 2: Optical Publishing, edited by Suzanne Ropiequet; published by Microsoft Press. Plenty of well-focused hard information. Not for the casual reader.

CD-ROM and Optical Publishing Systems, by Tony Hedley (Cimtech); published by Learned Information Ltd. Excellent and more or less up to date.

The CD-ROM Source Book, edited by Helgerson and Ennis; published by DDRI, 6609 Rosecroft Place, Falls Church, Virginia 22043, USA. Updated monthly.

CD-ROM Standards: The Book, by Julie B. Schwerin; published by Learned Information Ltd.

The Optical/Electronic Publishing Directory, by Richard A. Bowers; published by Learned Information Ltd.

Video Discs, Compact Discs and Digital Optical Disc Systems, by Tony Hedley (Cimtech)) published by Learned Information Ltd. Beginning to show its age but is still very useful.

Index